THE LEFT AND THE EROTIC

The Left
and the Erotic

edited by

EILEEN PHILLIPS

LAWRENCE AND WISHART
LONDON

Lawrence and Wishart Limited
39 Museum Street
London WC1A 1LQ

This edition first published 1983

0853155844

Photoset in North Wales by
Derek Doyle & Associates, Mold, Clwyd
Printed in Great Britain by
Camelot Press, Southampton

Contents

Acknowledgements

We are grateful to Michèle Roberts and her publishers for kind
permission to reprint her poems. *judith and delilah and me* and
Klevshaven first appeared in *Cutlasses and Earrings*, published
by Playbooks in 1977.
I am abroad in a strange land '*Women's entry into culture is
experienced as lack*', *memories of trees* and *punkroch; and Cocksparrow
sings* first appeared in *Licking the Bed Clean*, published by Teeth
Imprints in 1978.
unscientific is an unpublished manuscript.
The Knight Errant by Sir John Everett Millais is reproduced by
courtesy of the Tate Gallery, London.

Preface

It was perhaps the surprise of staring at a sea of 400 faces gathered for a workshop on 'The Left and the Erotic' at the Moving Left Show one Sunday morning in October 1982 which provided the conviction that a published discussion would be a useful vehicle for continuing the debate begun then. For some there was little to be astonished at in seeing the left using a Sunday morning to talk about rather than practice eroticism. Yet for most of us present in that sometimes tumultuous debate, it was an exciting moment. Moving sexual politics into the concerns of socialism seemed a victory, another recognition that the questions raised by feminism were not simply to be answered by the women's movement.

I would like to thank all those who participated in the workshop, both as part of the panel and as audience, who took part in discussions preceding it and who supported me through the nerve-wracking business of organising and then chairing a session I thought could easily degenerate into a blood-bath. I would also like to thank those at Lawrence & Wishart, particularly Stephen Hayward, who encouraged this book through to completion, sustaining the belief that however bizarre it seemed, the project was a worthwhile one. I am sure all the contributors would join with me in recognising the importance of those sisters, brothers and comrades whose politics have ensured a meaning for this collection of essays.

Finally I would like to thank Mandy, Naomi and Tricia who have lived with me and the book over the last year and provided the crucial mixture of laughter, tea and talking to see it through.

Eileen Phillips

Introduction: Libertarianism, 'Egotism' and Liberation

'I can't imagine anything less erotic than sitting on hard chairs in a smoky room trying to avoid the chairperson's eye when they're asking for volunteers to leaflet,' was one friend's reaction to the incongruous idea that there might be a relationship between the left and the erotic. 'Don't the left just deny the erotic?' she continued, adding that if it was the sex lives of comrades which was going to be revealed, quite frankly she could do without it. I share her reluctance to peruse a book filled with revelations such as 'true confessions of a trade unionist' or 'reds in the bed: the secret lives of communists'. So I can relieve (or disappoint) potential readers at the outset – this book is not a foray into the sexual imaginations of political activists. It is an attempt to talk a politics of sex, to explore possible connections between desires, fantasies, pleasures and the kinds of transformations in social relations which socialist convictions involve pursuing.

As such there are more questions raised than answers given. There is no aim to chase after the somewhat chilling spectre of socialist policy which legislates permissible and impermissible sexual behaviour. In 1915 Stella Browne, an active campaigner for abortion and birth control rights and a member of the Communist Party of Great Britain in its first two years, wrote warning of the consequences of socialist legislating about sex:

> I think no one who knows the 'personnel' of many social reform movements, can doubt that this is a very real danger. Persons of cold temperament have special aptitudes for much valuable work: they have their peculiar excellences, their precious achievements.

But they must not alone make the laws for more ardent natures.[1]

Rather than legislating behaviour, the essays in this collection at times nudge a toe gingerly into the debate over what might constitute sexual freedom, at others put their foot right in it. Hopefully they are provocative – the aim is to inspire further discussion, not to bring down an iron curtain on our so-called 'private lives'. All the writers have tried not to be mystifying, or at least be clear about when they themselves are mystified in relation to the often surprising features of sexuality and discussions surrounding it.

A significant omission from the contents of this book is any discussion of pornography. However, rather than this being a glaring oversight, it signals an important emphasis in the arena of debate chosen. Recently much feminist writing and activity have been devoted to arguments concerning the relation between pornography and rape and misogyny in general, or from another point of view in the debate – the possibility of constructing a feminist erotica. I would concur with the views expressed by Lesley Stern that anti-porn arguments which conflate power with violence and reduce sexism to sex, position the anti-porn movement as reactionary.

> If rape is the grand metaphor of oppression, then porn is the original sin. And the case for the prosecution rests in part on preserving the evidence of original sin.

This falls into the territory of the right where sex and violence are similarly untheorised, while being divided into the good and the bad –

> There is good sex, which unites and reproduces the family, and there is also legitimate violence, as exercised by the state through the military and the police forces, which unites the nation.[2]

But as well as providing the grounds for confusions with reactionary social ideologies, a focus on pornography pulls us away from the project of establishing strategies of pleasures, freedoms, desires. We remain caught in the noose of negative critiques of sexual relations, only able to speak the violence and degradation; we are silenced about the excitements or compulsions or delights of sensual existence. This collection of essays should be read as an attempt to seek political connections of change and challenge which point towards what could be out of what is, and not what most direfully and disablingly is.

The contributions are eclectic, encompassing topics as apparently wide apart as romance, nineteenth century imperialist male sexuality, a discussion of the past of the British Communist Party in relation to sexual politics and representation of sex in literature. The authors, too, are mixed in the everyday use of the term. Men have been included, not only if they are gay men (and therefore understood by some as fit to carry the honourable badge of feminism). Heterosexual men write here as part of 'The Left' and as part of an insistence that it is not the exclusive task of women to integrate an understanding of our sexual and political practices. For too long women have been simultaneously elevated and peripheralised as guardians of sexual politics – this stands as an attempt to inch a way out of the ghetto.

To take up the initial question of denial and the purported failure of the left to do other than suppress the erotic – there have been political precedents for attempting an integration of sexual issues into the concerns of anti-capitalist movements. Chronologically, the closest was in the late sixties when sexual permissiveness was elevated to a strategy, a politics of challenge to repression. That repression was understood as empowering the violence of imperialism, consumer capitalism and family life. Organising against the Vietnam war, racism and parental control were all part of the same defiance of the older generation's submission to their lack of freedom. Daniel Cohn-Bendit, one of the major ideologues of May '68 in Paris, poured passionate scorn on the 'old left's' approach to sexual and economic matters, which he understood as inextricably linked. Stalinist bureaucrats and liberals alike, he fumed, reduced

> the evils of capitalism to economic injustice ... And when they
> extend their criticism of capitalism to other fields, they still imply

that everything would be solved by a fairer distribution of wealth. The sexual problems of youth and the difficulties of family life are ignored – all that apparently needs to be solved is the problem of prostitution.

Whereas the generation of '68 firmly believed that:

> If a social organisation is repressive it will be so on the sexual and cultural no less than on the economic planes.[3]

Obviously there is a fatal inadequacy in any analysis which reduces all politics of sexuality to the problem of prostitution which it then 'explains' by the economic necessities which force women into this sort of occupation. It is an economism which reduces sexuality to the problem of capitalism's ability to make everything, including sex, into a commodity which can be bought and sold on the market. As Mary McIntosh points out, there are more power relations operating than purely economic ones:

> A common view, that of the 'double standard' of sexual morality, is that frequenting prostitutes, perhaps more than any other forms of promiscuity is forgiveable in the male, while being a prostitute, again perhaps more than any other form of promiscuity, is totally reprehensible in the female.[4]

But what was to replace an economist strategy which ignored sexual power relations? For the youth of '68 an anti-repression politics meant engaging in activities such as 'The Battle of the Dormitories'. They began a sex-education campaign on the Nanterre campus, which as Cohn-Bendit approvingly reported:

> culminated in male students forcibly entering the women's hostels and after this many of the petty restrictions surrounding these bastions of French purity and chastity were repealed.[5]

Not a whisper about how the female students felt about these 'liberationist activities' – we are left to presume that eventually they would be grateful to these male warriors for saving them from the backwardness of 'chastity', or even worse, 'frigidity'.

Meanwhile, across the Atlantic Ocean, Stokely Carmichael was making his infamous statement about the only position for women in the black power movement being 'prone'. Women began to protest that desire was not so innocent as the Paris students were proclaiming, that there was a world of difference between an easy lay and a free woman. And in between was the construction of woman as the object of male pleasure/approval/disapproval; instead of woman being the subject, the one acting out a desire, she was the more or less useful tool for male sexual gratification. As Cynthia Cockburn has described recently:

> men want women's sexuality as free currency. They want women to be like the communal bicycles in the Amsterdam of the libertarian revolt of the 1960s, there to be picked up, ridden and laid aside by anyone at any time.[6]

I remember, as a wide-eyed teenager in 1971, visiting some ex-students in York who shared a house and were to teach us the rudiments of street theatre. I wasn't quite sure at the time what living communally involved – did that mean everybody moved in and out of each other's beds, and, if so, would we have to join in? Feeling tempted to run away I argued with myself about the fears that these terribly sophisticated, mature, cool people seemed to be provoking in me. Was I just a prude or was there something I had a right to feel uneasy about? Buried deep in my sleeping bag, attempting to simulate the sleep of the dead in the living room that people hadn't yet left, I listened to a conversation about a woman who had just joined the household. One of the men who had aimed in my direction a number of cold stares which looked right through me, was asking in a weary voice: 'Has anyone had her yet? Does anyone know what she's like to fuck?' I hadn't discovered the language of feminism then, but I knew immediately that there was no sort of sexual freedom that I myself wanted in this exchange of women by men. I wondered what the women in the room felt, but I never gathered up courage to ask. It was to be a few years before the Women's Liberation Movement was strong enough to ensure that such blatant expressions of male hatred and contempt of women would not go unchallenged.

So, despite the strength of libertarian ideologies which interpreted any resistance women showed towards this type of sexual activity as their clinging onto reactionary mores, women did break away from male definitions of sexuality. The WLM grasped the nettle of an apparent contradiction – demanding women's rights to sexual pleasure outside the controlling structures of the family, while asserting that heterosexual relations were a crucial element in confining women to a private and powerless sphere. As we shall see later, that dilemma has created problems for feminists which in more recent times have manifested themselves as bitter divisions within the movement. For some women the obvious, and they argue, necessary solution is to shun heterosexuality. They believe that all sexual engagement with men has to be equated with a perverse desire that women persist in exhibiting 'to love their enemy'. For others, that very persistence (whether experienced personally or not) means that a politics of struggle rather than condemnation has to be pursued if feminism is to have a resonance for more than a tiny group of the dedicated.

Instead of fixing women as victims of male exploitation and heaping blame onto the heads of male predators (a blame which spills over onto the woman if she 'knows' about male domination and yet might still on occasion hold a man's hand) we need to look for the contradictions in sexual relations. Resolving these may loosen the structures of power and domination which inform love, desire and sexual activity and provide a political, rather than moral framework for action. For instance, a woman may feel claustrophobic and secure in her marriage – rather than insisting that the 'trap' is more 'real' than the support, we have to seek out material alternatives offering emotional and economic possibilities that allow the choice of independence to be other than a leap into a terrifying abyss of isolation and poverty. Contradictions need unlocking rather than burying – banishing men to the realm of 'untouchables' cannot create sexual democracy; neither can it subvert the class and racial dominations which socialists recognise as integrated with questions of sexual power relations.

One of the obvious features of attempts to practice a sexual politics is that it involves challenging ways of living as much as campaigning for women's rights. It is a life-style politics, an attempt to create alternatives in the here and now, rather than 'after the revolution'. In this context we have to understand the legacy of the sixties as a strange one for the WLM. On the one hand there was the anger at men's expectations of women's sexual availability which helped to fuel those first moves to organise as women. On the other, libertarian politics had flung open the door of the home and the bedroom and said what went on there mattered. These things mattered not just because people are unhappy or happy in their living situations and sex lives, but because class society is shored up and reproduced in these places which the ruling classes want to guard with the label of privacy.

Private lives were public questions according to the youth of '68. Some even considered that the desire for privacy in any form was in itself a reactionary one. The Beatles song 'Why don't we do it in the road?' spoke to the exuberance of young people who both shouted out for public spectacle and equated the wish for privacy with inhibition and repression. And of course feminists were insisting that private lives were political, that it was within the sanctuary of the home that women were crucially confined into their subordination. Feminists also held that the key to change was recognising that the humiliations and denials suffered there were not individual problems. It was because they were experienced as such that women were kept quiet or sent slowly round the bend. By breaking down the walls of their isolation women could discover how many others felt the same way and become empowered to challenge their oppression.

It was a very different power structure that women were exposing in personal life, one in which men rather than the bourgeoisie were benefiting. But this politics shared an important understanding with the libertarians, that is, politics doesn't stop outside the factory gates or away from the institutions of the state. Neither does it stop at demanding a bigger share of the cake, with a struggle for 'more' so that

women would move from having less than men to having
equal portions. The cake's recipe itself was being questioned –
the social organisation of work, procreation, sex, culture,
needed new forms which could construct freedom rather than
power to dominate, development instead of denial,
co-operation rather than suppression, and not more of the
same for the deprived.

There have of course been historical precedents within the
socialist tradition for visionary politics, ones which earned the
label 'utopianism' in the nineteenth century. Barbara Taylor in
Eve and the New Jerusalem gives a fascinating account of
attempts to found communities which concentrated on doing
away with marriage-ties and creating new forms of love based
on women's emancipation as much as on bringing to an end
the economic exploitation of capitalism. She argues that the
Marxist critique of the non-materialist character of these
socialisms lost touch with the quest for women's liberation
from male sexual control. By locating the focus of struggle in
the harsh realities of factory production and the possibility of
the industrial proletariat rebelling, socialists began to turn
away from considering changes in the relations between the
sexes as central to any new social order emerging.[7]

The depth of concern about women's subordination
exhibited by early nineteenth century socialists, shows itself in
a funny little book called *The Strike of a Sex*. In it the author, a
participant in the Oneida community in America, argues
passionately about the damage to women's health and freedom
caused by forced and numerous pregnancies. He reveals the
secret of happiness for both men and women – the Zaragossa
Principle. Essentially this involves men developing self-control
to the point where they can copulate without ejaculating. Men
learn true desire rather than animal lust and women are freed
from the prison of continuous and often fatal child-bearing.
Given the centrality accorded to the male orgasm in
contemporary sexual practices, it appears extraordinary that
this could ever have been suggested as a method of
contraception. But equally interesting is its attempt to present
advantages for both sexes in changed sexual relations. It reads
naively as it simply wishes away the issue of male power, but it

does suggest the existence of a way of thinking within radicalism that could have presumed women's emancipation as a liberation for all. This can be contrasted with recent efforts by socialists to accommodate feminism through adding 'women's rights' to the political agenda. Even if these demands move up the list of priorities from a precarious position at the bottom, they do not redefine socialism as a project which seeks to transorm all social relations, including those which are sexual.

Are there other parts of the socialist tradition that can be usefully examined in the light of feminism's discussion of 'private lives'? And might that examination provide a foundation to be built on, rather than re-asserting the necessity for breaking away from a male-dominated revolutionary culture? In 1978 I finished reading Chernyshevsky's story *What Is To Do Done? Tales About New People*, written in 1862. My imagination was captured by the message of 'free love' spoken both by the characters and the novelist's direct address to the reader. The vision of how the 'new people' might conduct their affairs encompassed a husband facilitating the love affair between his friend and his wife, the woman living an emotional, intellectual and financial independence within the subsequent second marriage, and ultimately a faith in the possibility of a society in which there would be work without compulsion and love without possession.

It was forty years later that Lenin borrowed from the title for his book about the revolutionary party and the comrade's role in pushing forward the struggle, forcing the contradictions to maturity. Lenin's 'answer' to Chernyshevsky equally fed my romantic aspirations for revolution and the role of the revolutionary. The years I had spent involved in the WLM may have convinced me that Leninism wasn't enough to transform the oppressions and exploitations lived out in sexual relations, but my allegiance to the all-seeing, courageous, revolutionary hero, whose heart was in social change rather than personal gain, had hardly been shaken. (Fortunately the fantasy figure was a fairly androgynous one so I could on occasion slip myself into the picture.) But although Lenin may have believed that his strategy for revolution gave a grounding of

Chernyshevsky's utopianism by providing the material conditions for the 'new people' to exist, there were certain crucial denials of liberty that remained unaddressed.

I began to toy with the idea of defining a 'revolutionary morality', a set of principles and understandings which would provide the political activist with the means to accelerate the resolution of contradictions in the area of life deemed 'private' by the major part of the socialist tradition. Just as Lenin had prescribed the necessities and duties of the comrade in relation to the masses and to movements which aimed to eradicate economic exploitation and create the conditions for political liberty, perhaps it would be possible to construct a blueprint for action in comrades' 'personal' lives. And this wouldn't simply be a code of behaviour, do's and don'ts which might differ in content from bourgeois morality but would be essentially the same in their denial and constriction of behaviour. Rather the morality would be directed towards change, not accepting a core of immutable 'human nature' which no politics can address, but instead seeing the potential for and working towards free and equal relationships.

However, there is a crucial difference between Lenin's sphere of class struggle with the space it can create for the romance of a selfless hero, and 'personal' life which every individual has. The problems experienced in the latter, the struggles for equal power and control, for an end to one person's subordination to another, are not ones that can be displaced into the abstract and perhaps safer arena of problems facing the masses. They are suffered, often in an intensely painful way, by the individual concerned, experienced as problems of the 'me' and 'I' who is struggling with them. Whatever the belief of the comrade that a communist society would benefit her/him, and alleviate oppressions that she/he suffered, both the suffering and the benefit often appear to take a more philosophical form, or at least be more indirect when compared to the burdens, fears and dominations experienced in so-called private life. It was almost as if the revolutionary I read Lenin as describing could rise above a personal, individual existence and perceive the necessary solutions as embedded in changing such impersonal things as the bourgeois state or class relations.

In a way it was this that made Leninism, even moved from its context in pre-revolutionary Russia to a 1970s Britain, more attractive than a Labourism which understood political change as about advancing the immediate, already-constituted interests of the working class. Lenin talked a politics of power relations and contradictions which the workers, if left to their own devices, would not discover and resolve. Later I translated this as élitism, but at the time I contrasted it favourably to a populism which saw the working class as already progressive, already the agent for social change, as long as it steadily pursued the advance of its own interests. In the latter version of socialist politics there was no question mark hanging over what these interests were, over whether male and female working class interests could be in conflict, no need to understand the working class as caught in contradictory allegiances to both hierarchichal power and collective resistance – the working class 'suffered' (whether expressed as deprivation or exploitation hardly shifted the political analysis) and therefore changed the world. For Lenin suffering did not produce the dynamic of change, neither by propelling the oppressed worker towards revolution, nor by activating the sympathies of the bourgeois and so encouraging a fervour for socialism.

As long as the Leninist revolutionary was locked into responding 'personally' she/he would be like the young comrade in Brecht's play *The Measures Taken* who, being moved by pity and anger at the plight of the masses, hinders the cause of revolution. By helping rather than organising the workers, by giving the worker shoes rather than getting the workers to strike in demand of shoes from their employer, the comrade only ensured that a power relation, a situation of dependency rather than equality was reproduced. Or as Brecht puts it in his poem 'The Joy of Giving':

What rose is fairer than the face
Of one whom we play the donors?
Behold his hands, o highest bliss
Encumbered with our gracious favours.

Was it possible to translate the sort of revolutionary activity I understood as needed for overcoming bourgeois class power into the sphere of the personal? A friend wrote to me around this time in which I was moving somewhat reluctantly towards relinquishing my construction of the Leninist hero, saying:

> Lenin's model is not very useful for a morality. I think selfishness is a much better one. We tend to hate selfishness and think of men going to the pub without a thought, or getting sex when they want, never mind the pain or tiredness. But that comes through power exercised in many ways, one of which is the woman (in this case) not wishing to be selfish. If our affairs were conducted in the great spirit of selfishness then they'd be endlessly negotiated. Which sounds fair enough to me. Everything *is* conducted in the spirit of selfishness but because of our morality we want to keep quiet about that, because we want to seem nicer people.

There is an interesting passage in Chernyshevsky showing an exchange between Lopukhow (the husband) and Kirsanov (the friend) which deals with this notion of selfishness or egotism. Lopukhow, having perceived that his wife Vera and his friend love each other, and that each is trying to suppress the knowledge of this from both Lopukhov and the other, engages in a 'theoretical discussion' with Kirsanov. By talking of a hypothetical triangular situation, he communicates to Kirsanov both that he knows of the affair and that he does not wish to prevent it occurring. Kirsanov refused the invitation to declare his love for his friend's wife but eventually agrees to recommence visiting the couple's house as long as he is never left alone with Vera. The dialogue is conducted in the spirit of rationalism and altruism, each concerned to act for the other's emotional well-being. However the novelist points out that Lopukhov could have examined his own actions in relation to his wife and seen that

> One renounces that which is lost, and egoism so shapes things that one sets himself up as a man performing an heroic act.

He had failed to let his friend know that his wife was unhappy in her marriage and had instead presented himself as his friend's benefactor. Kirsanov in turn could have reflected on his response to the initiative:

> I want to preserve my place, to rest on my laurels, and I preach that one has no right to compromise a woman's tranquillity. ... I refuse to yield to the first word of invitation ... that I may not be deprived of the sweet joy which my noble way of acting causes me.[8]

As the story unfolds we witness the 'sweet joy' of nobility giving way to the 'sweet joy' of passion and the pretence of self-sacrifice to the reality of loss. But what Chernyshevsky appears concerned to show is that in this rational approach to sexual relations, with its attempt to construct freedom rather than obligation, independence rather than possession, the outcome can only be progressive if the calls of 'egotism' are listened to.

Perhaps this sounds a surprising perspective on socialist ideology, which is usually understood as holding that individualism is a creation of the conflict and competition within capitalism and will be superseded by a collectivism built out of the co-operation and solidarity of socialism. But the crucial understanding that Chernyshevsky wanted to express was that independence, most importantly women's independence in relation to men, was the only basis for the co-operation and mutual aid which socialist society could create. If a woman is dependant on a man, if a man sees a woman as his property, then there can be no freedom, but only jealousy and unhappiness. As one of the 'new men' in the story puts it:

> [Jealousy] is a distorted feeling, a false feeling, an abominable feeling, it is a phenomenon of our existing order of things, based on the same idea that prevents me from permitting anyone to wear my linen or smoke my pipe: it is a result of considering one's companion as an object that one has appropriated.[9]

And as the heroine muses after her decision to study medicine, taken when she realised that despite her affection and allegiance to Kirsanov (now her husband) and his reciprocation of the committment, she was feeling depressed and insecure:

> In a few years I shall get a foothold. That is a great thought. There is no complete happiness without complete independence. Poor women that you are, how few of you enjoy this happiness.[10]

It is this sort of reasoning which might explain such things as the change, at first sight perverse, of title of the British suffragette magazine from *The Freewoman* to *The Egoist*. Rather than reflecting the anti-feminist belief that any free woman must be a selfish one, putting her own interests before those of her husband, her children or her parents, it suggests that freedom is built from a self-centredness which involves neither being in dependence on, or in manipulation of, others.

This picture that Chernyshevsky paints of a new society in which self-denial is articulated as a perhaps quaint, but definitely historical quasi-religious practice, is above all a rationalist one. There is order in personal dealings, an ultimate belief in the possibility of rational dialogue and decision, as long as the 'truth' of people's conflicting desires is confronted. There are echoes of this faith in the present day American feminist Adrienne Rich's writing. In *Women and Honor* she tackles the issue of lying and powerlessness:

> In the struggle for survival we tell lies. To bosses, to prison guards, the police, men who have power over us, who legally own us and our children, lovers who need us as proof of their manhood. There is a danger run by all powerless people: that we forget we are lying, or that lying becomes a weapon we carry over into relationships with people who do not have power over us.

And to avoid this, women have to be able to encounter the pain or anger of another, rather than attempting to use lies or silences to cover up the conflict:

> The liar may resist confrontation, denying that she lied. Or she may use other language: forgetfulness, privacy, the protection of someone else. Or she may bravely declare herself a coward. This allows her to go on lying since that is what cowards do. She does

not say, *I was afraid*, since this would open the question of what is actually feared. She may say *I didn't want to cause pain*. What she really did not want is to have to deal with the other's pain. The lie is a short-cut through another's personality.[11]

But in this utopia, 'truth-telling' requires only daring – although Rich recognises that there is more than one truth, she retains a belief in only one self. The unitary 'I' can make its confession to the other 'I's and set in motion the resolution of conflicts between them. There remains no space for unconscious desires, for contradictions and diversities within the number of selves each person may inhabit at once. Subjectivity as expressed in the diary or letter, or speech of the consciousness raising group, is not then seen as constructed – as long as the person is not 'lying' we are bearing witness to the truth.

This is particularly important when we face the arena of the erotic where 'truth' is often least transparent (think of those surprising dreams we wake from in embarrassed astonishment) and where conflicts with another, or other kinds of obstacles in the way of sexual activity or passion may be precisely what constructs the desire. Being unattainable makes the object of desire all the more compellingly attractive; keeping a pleasure 'secret' can often be what keeps it as a pleasure; running the risk of 'being found out' or the danger of the partner of a lover attempting revenge can intensify the excitement, promote the sense of the overwhelming nature of the passion which flies in the face of convention, breaks all the rules, because the lovers are incapable of 'denying' it.

A scenario such as this may explain Chernyshevsky writing in another moment:

> Away with erotic problems. The modern reader has no interest in them. He is concerned with the question of perfecting the administration and the judicial system, with financial questions, with the problem of liberating the peasant.

The public success, both at the time of publication and now, of *What Is To Be Done?* suggests Chernyshevsky made an incorrect estimate of the interests of both male and female readers. But the problem remains of how to develop a continuum from the rational ordering of a socialist economy, which overcomes the excesses and chaos of the market and provides democratic control, to a rationalist sexual politics when sex and the erotic appear to thrive on irrationalism, on excess and chaos and on lack of control.

It is a particularly acute problem for feminists when attempting to develop practices which assert women as sexual subjects, rather than objects. A younger brother of a friend of mine once asked me why it was that feminists slept with other women's men. To answer in the rhetoric of a woman's sexual autonomy, of a refusal to admit one person's possession by another, was possible but felt peculiarly unsatisfactory. It is an uncomfortable position to take, insisting that another woman's hurt is neither caused by you, nor your concern, when the politics of feminism speak of women's solidarity and overcoming the competition between women over men. This becomes an even more uneasy stance when the experience of jealousy and vulnerability within a supposedly monogamous sexual relationship can hardly be described as a historical residue when it comes to examining your own experience. And what if you know that being the 'other woman' as opposed to the wife, in itself feeds the thrills, while you avoid the trap of marital dependency (along with its apparent boredom)? Choosing to be 'a mistress' does not equate with engaging in guerrilla warfare against the institution of marriage – far from it, the wife/mistress dualism is inextricable. This is recognised by Ruth Dickson in an exceptionally nasty book entitled *Married Men Make the Best Lovers*, in which she advises women to take the precaution of making friends with the deceived wife in order to sustain the possibility of an illicit relationship which provides her with all the attentions the man fails to give his wife.

And if we look at the 'wife' side of the coin (I mean by wife not the legal term, but rather a positioning within a long-term heterosexual or lesbian relationship) then the problem of jealousy enters in an extremely destructive form. As Jill Lewis puts it:

there is the propensity in our gendered unconscious, mothered into existence in the isolated, patriarchal nuclear family, to quest for the unique affirmation that one loving relationship can give.[12]

Obviously jealousy and the desire to be the most important person in the world to someone, is not a problem only experienced by women. In fact it could be argued that men, through the power over women that is open to them, through their reluctance either to recognise or accept defeat, act as the more jealous sex. A woman I know has recently given up an attempt to carry on, openly, a second sexual relationship because the man she lives with took to coming home from work unexpectedly in the middle of the day. I find it hard to imagine a woman pursuing a similar course of self-preservation as this man did – after all even if a woman wanted to keep a constantly watchful eye on her man's movements, she would find it extremely difficult to do so practically – let alone managing to withstand the man's fury at being tailed to and from work, the pub or football match.

There is a similar argument in the analysis derived from Freud's presentation of the different entry of men and women into the 'law of the father', which sees men as looking for their mothers in their lovers, while women remain unsure whether they are looking for their fathers or their mothers. For heterosexual men, the bonding with another is less ambiguous, so the potential for jealousy and possession expands dramatically, unimpeded by gender confusions over having first learnt an unassailable love and completely satisfying self-affirmation from the mother.

However the woman who is confined to the home with children, who may be working part-time but is not economically independent, is hardly in a position to assert an autonomous sexuality. And she is certainly extremely vulnerable if it appears that her perhaps sole source of financial, child-care and even emotional support is threatened by the man's involvement in the excitement of 'an affair'. Wilhelm Reich may have been able to argue that the hatred, submerged or otherwise, he saw between family members, the 'forced affection and sticky dependence', was due to the woman relinquishing sexual gratification for a maternal relationship:

> One of the main difficulties was the inability of the woman ... to give up the slave-like protection of the family and substitute gratification which lay in their domination over the children ... The woman, because her whole life was sexually empty and economically dependent, had made the upbringing of her children the content of her life.[13]

But blaming the claustrophobia of family life on the woman's giving up of sexual freedom ends up as moralism rather than a politics, and a pretty one-sided moral condemnation when the benefits accruing to the man from this situation remain unspoken. After all, he can have his cake and eat it too – retaining his role as 'father' without the curtailment of his freedom that being a mother demands, having a faithful wife who doesn't threaten his vanity or psychic security by finding pleasure in other sexual relations. And even if he feels trapped, for him there is always the spice of adultery, which may even become more intoxicating if a measure of guilt is added to it, while there is little fear of the kind of social censure meted out to unfaithful wives and mothers.

Choosing to be an autonomous sexual agent as opposed to either a wife or mistress, remains an elusive, fantastical idea. Looking at Ursula LeGuin's book *The Dispossessed* as an example of utopian fiction which visualises a sexually free society, it is interesting to see how thoroughly this is tied to a breaking down of the institution of heterosexuality and of 'mothering' as the sole preserve and duty of women. On the planet Urras both men and women may choose to balance the demands of work with those of parental care. And although 'partnerships' can be formed which may last a person's lifetime, there is both the possibility and expectation of other sexual encounters with either men or women. In the realms of science fiction jealousy and possessive feelings between lovers, or parents and children, can be imagined away. Male sexual abuse of women, any form of sexual exploitation, can become strange social practices of another planet resembling Earth (there are no words for 'rape' or 'to fuck someone' in the language spoken on Urras).

Interestingly enough the biological facts of procreation and childbirth remain the same. Shulamith Firestone, whose book *The Dialectic of Sex* was an important focus of debate in the WLM of the early seventies, understood the biological basis of reproduction as the crucial factor in determining women's oppression. She prophesied that until babies were grown in test tubes rather than in a woman's body, there could be no end to male control of female sexuality and identity. As such the book has been criticised for arguing a kind of technological and biological determinism. But in *The Dispossessed* there is no resort to this kind of scientistic solution – as Shevek, its hero, explains to an interrogator from Annarres (Earth) who is shocked and terrified by the lack of sexual divisions on Shevek's planet, that genital sexual differences which create variations in sexual practices and in procreation are not obliterated. 'That would be a waste of good equipment', is Shevek's rationalistic and amused response.

To get back to the planet Earth and political strategies rather than fictions, it seems clear that any attempt to create sexual freedom has to be linked to challenges to 'motherhood' and 'fatherhood' as at present constructed. Common-sense views of the world might readily claim that the contraceptive pill gave women freedom. And although medical dangers hardly inscribe it as the safe way to contraceptive security, when reading descriptions of the horrors women have suffered in the past, forced into repeated pregnancy, I breathe a measured sigh of relief at the predicaments we face today. But some women also want to be mothers, and even if they are able to control when and how many children they have, are they then pushed into taking the choice of a maternal rather than a sexual existence?

Perhaps this dilemma facing women is peculiarly one of white culture – the older man pursuing the increasingly younger woman as his female contemporary becomes more firmly assigned to the 'mother' rather than 'lover' category of his sexual imagination: the older woman who is a mother resigning herself to the social denial and rejection of her sexuality through giving priority to her love for her children. I can only really speculate about other ethnic cultures, but I was challenged by Gloria Joseph's discussion of black female sexuality which stands alongside the white feminist perspective of Jill Lewis in their book *Common Differences: conflicts in black and white feminist perspectives*. Joseph describes how within black communities there may be a simultaneous proscribing of extra-marital sex for young girls and women, while any child which is the product of the forbidden activity will be welcomed by everyone, including the minister's wife. And once a mother, a woman will not then automatically become re-defined as asexual or directing her energies to her child as opposed to a present or potential lover. This appears to be linked to a widening of the basis for child-care, both through an extended family and via the network of support and interest in young additions to a community tied together by the economic and political facts of racial oppression. There also seems to be a significance in the economically independent roles women often play – girls see their mothers having jobs which support the family, and although this may mean women work fantastically hard, often combining the demands of badly paid jobs with those of large households, there remain material conditions for a certain form of women's autonomy which can include sexual independence.

When Joseph discusses 'sexual politics' she presents a picture of 'realpolitik', a terrain of game-playing and negotiations in sexual interaction, which puts a different emphasis to much of recent feminist polemics:

> She [the young female] soon realises the games, 'sexual politics', that are going on … For the female the game-playing is face-saving. If she gives in without the 'games', she is considered a whore. Males play all sorts of games to keep the female believing she is the one. For example, when they go away, they will remind themselves to call So-and-so at a certain time to demonstrate how much they care. Notes for a trip: blue suit, shoe brush, *call Millie*, Brut, toothbrush, *call Marie*, comb, deodorant, *call Sally*. She is just another item that is needed for his care. He may make the call in between fucking rounds, but that doesn't matter. The female will feel cared for.

The 'games' in which it takes two to play (with of course different rules, expectations of 'winning' and 'losing', understandings of success and failure) could be stopped. For instance:

> Should the games be stopped and the women simply say 'I'm in this for a good screw just like you, so let's stop with the games', we would have a new situation.[14]

This is a rhetoric which talks of a mutual engagement in the 'politics' rather than showing women as victims to male aggression or seduction. Women are still understood as playing games with dice loaded against them, but because they are involved actively in the set-ups, there is a space constructed for women's refusal to play any more, or their demand for new rules. As such it holds a greater promise for change than an analysis which locks women into a scenario of eternal abuse and degradation.

To turn to a different ethnic community, the Asian one, one of the important points Amrit Wilson makes in her book *Asian Women: Finding a Voice*, is that Asian women who come to Britain can suddenly find themselves terribly isolated within a hostile community, having left behind the community of women created by the extreme sexual segregation they have been living. So integration into a more mixed society, in terms of both race and gender, has contradictory effects. A woman may acquire the freedom of being away from the potentially despotic control of her husband's mother while losing a source of knowledge and care in relation to her sexual identity, gained from the women she used to spend her time with.

Similarly in relation to breaking away from the practice of arranged marriages: if the 'liberation' takes the form of love-marriages, it is not clear that one form of tyranny has not been substituted for another. There is an argument sometimes made that Western ideologies of love and passion locate its possibility only outside marriage, while at the same time firmly asserting marriage as the desirable outcome of love. But if the erotic and the sexual can only exist where there are obstacles to be overcome, where the barriers and forces that pull people apart from each other are exactly what fuels their desire, then Western forms of marriage are doomed never to incorporate the sexual. And surprising though it seems to us, the oldest and perhaps most famous celebration of the erotic, the *Kama Sutra*, was specifically written for married people, and so reflects an Eastern ideology that the erotic can be cultivated within partnerships, rather than be found only in forbidden, elusive and transient sexual encounters.

These remarks on different cultures should only be read as tentative ones. But it seems important to attempt to place in context our understanding of the erotic in order to help refine our politics as well as our visions. I am not suggesting we need a kind of anthropology of sex, so we can choose which variety of ideological construction suits our taste. But rather, as part of a project of avoiding the final resting place being a conviction of the natural, essential, and therefore unchangeable, human urges present in sex, we need to consider differences that do exist, and try to trace these to lived cultural, political and economic processes.

To return to the initial discussion of feminist break-away from libertarian ideology which masks women's subordination in the cloak of 'un-repressed' sexual activity – to some of us it seems we've reached an impasse. The possibility of erotic pleasure, desire and of sex drown in a sea of knowledge of the power relations which underpin them. And this in a time when sexology, sex-manuals, sex-aids, the popular press drum through our waking moments with today's messianic messages: 'sex is good for you', 'orgasm can be, and ought to be, reached by all', 'strengthen the self with a healthy, active sex-life'.

For women the 'discovery' of the clitoral orgasm is presumed to have opened the doors of equality in sexual pleasure, of woman as a sexual partner who enjoys it as much as the man does. The contradictory nature of this 'advance' out of ignorance, in that women now become required to be orgasmic if a man is to feel sexually adequate, remains unspoken, as does the territory which women's bodies are endlessly forced to provide for the latest break-through in sexual knowledge. Judith Williamson argues compellingly in

relation to the most recent proclamation of sexual equality –
the discovery of the 'G Spot', which is described as located
somewhere in the vagina and which triggers off ejaculation and
orgasm for women:

> Our bodies become a form of fruit-machine, to be played on for
> pleasures: women can have different kinds of orgasms, multiple
> orgasms, plateaux, climaxes, ejaculation, you name it. But how
> about desire? – without which the G Spot is as useful as a hole in
> the head, and which equally can turn the nape of your neck or the
> back of your hand into a sexual explosion. But it is always as if
> men have desire. Women have 'pleasure' – usually given by a
> man.[15]

So the project of gaining women's pleasure, even when
described as depending on women's freedom from the family,
can still return to woman as other, passive, dependent on the
donor. It appears that desire is the crucial factor, the pin which
holds the edifice of male domination together. Pull out the pin
and the whole lot might collapse. By attempting an answer to
what it is for a woman to desire, we may be confronting the
complexity of power relations across gender, race and class,
rather than descending into naivety.

Because it is clear that the erotic, and changes in our erotic
lives, cannot be pursued in the name of 'equality' of male and
female sexual pleasure. Neither can a sexual politics stake out
an area separate from, autonomous of, other social and
economic changes. As Stella Browne put it:

> I do not think that any intelligent, humane and self-respecting
> attitude towards sex is generally possible, without great economic
> changes; and responsible education in the laws of sex, and a much
> wider co-operation and companionship between men and
> women, wholly * apart from erotic relations, are equally
> necessary.[16]

In terms of divisions within feminism between women who
choose lesbianism in order to defy male domination and
women, heterosexual or lesbian, who argue against a politics
of voluntarism and male banishment, there have been valiant

efforts made to heal the breach.[17] By arguing that pleasure for women is located in the clitoris, penetration can become unnecessary, irrational, an excess. Lesbian and heterosexual women can unite in a celebration of the clitoris and so turn the tables on male demands, control, desire. But this is a behaviourism which ignores desire as itself often unnecessary, irrational, an excess – and also compelling. When going to meet the desired one, we can be sweating, our legs trembling, our heart beating fast – in fact behaviourally we can be exhibiting the symptoms of fear. Yet it feels exciting as well as scary, the very strangeness producing a peculiar sort of clarity which often eludes us in many other activities of daily life.

Paradoxically it is hard to speak a language of freedom when dealing with emotions and fantasies which seem to drive the individual relentlessly in the pursuit of the object of desire. At the same time, if the context is one of obligation or coercion then desire vanishes, unable to sustain itself on demands for attention, as opposed to gratuitous offerings. It is here, with contradictions such as these, that the struggle for change has to be waged. Power being crucially exercised in sexuality gives us the chance of reconstructing personal relations, a reconstruction which will include many levels of complexity: physical, intellectual, familial, economic.

We have within the socialist tradition practices and understandings which can help as well as hinder us. Marge Piercy expresses well the ambivalence present in our relationship to history:

> The past leads to us if we force it to
> Otherwise it contains us
> in its asylum with no gates.
> We make history or it
> makes us.

We have also the need to transform our visions and our strategies so as to address a politics of freedom which does not relegate the personal and the sexual to a space where angels fear to tread and fools rush in. Perhaps by being angels and fools simultaneously we can move out of the impasse and look forward to the new world we are trying to create.

References

1 Sheila Rowbotham, *A New World for Women: Stella Brown – Socialist Feminist*, Pluto Press, 1977, p.94.
2 Lesley Stern, 'The Body as Evidence: a critical review of the pornography problematic', in *Screen*, Vol. 23, No. 5, pp. 51-52.
3 Daniel Cohn-Bendit, *Obsolete Communism: The Left-Wing Alternative*, Penguin, 1968, pp. 103-4.
4 Mary McIntosh, 'Who needs prostitutes? The ideology of male needs', in Smart & Smart (eds.) *Women, Sexuality and Social Control*, Routledge, 1978, p. 56.
5 Cohn-Bendit, op.cit., p. 29.
6 Cynthia Cockburn, *Brothers: male domination and technological change*, Pluto Press, 1983, p. 185.
7 Barbara Taylor, *Eve and the New Jerusalem*, Virago, 1983.
8 Nikolai Chernyshevsky, *What Is To Be Done? Tales About the New People,* Virago, 1982, pp. 209-10.
9 Ibid., p. 255.
10 Ibid., p. 299.
11 Adrienne Rich, *Women and Honor*, Onlywomen Press, 1979.
12 Gloria I. Joseph and Jill Lewis, *Common Differences: Conflicts In Black and White Feminist Perspectives*, Anchor Press, 1981, p. 263.
13 Wilhelm Reich, *The Sexual Revolution*, Vision Press, 1969, p. 168.
14 Joseph and Lewis, op.cit., p. 218.
15 Judith Williamson, 'Seeing Spots', *City Limits*, 25 March 1983.
16 Sheila Rowbotham, op.cit., p.91.
17 Bea Campbell and Anna Coote, *Sweet Freedom*, Picador, 1982.

Elizabeth Wilson

A New Romanticism

Rumour has it that there is a new fashion for romantic love. For long dismissed as uncool, a generation of radicals had rejected it in favour of sexual freedom, a generation of feminists because it symbolized passive enslavement to the masterful male. It was irrational, and must therefore be wrong.

In the spring of 1982, a feminist conference on sexuality was held at Barnard College, New York City. In a workshop on 'politically incorrect' sexuality, women described what turned them on. One after another described desires so exquisitely specific that my own seemed formless by comparison. I did not shudder with ecstasy at the thrill of a silk dress caressing my skin; did not drool at the word 'discipline' or melt at the sight of a jackboot, nor, if I did, would I define my sexual being, and more, my whole identity, in terms of that one desire. I could never have turned my person into a perambulating invitation by using the American sexual codes in which the placing of keys or different coloured handkerchiefs on the left or right side of the body announces to the world the wearer's preference for passive or active sex, for fellatio, shit or voyeurism.

Astonishment that women could define themselves and their sexual natures in terms of a single sexual act, a fetish or accessory, must have been general, for at times there were nervous explosions of laughter – the kind of laughter that masks both fear and longing. How enviable were these women who could announce the most bizarre desire with equanimity. Many of us, surely, would have been too shy or too proud, too fearful of ridicule or rejection to admit to such outlandish needs.

The possibility of rejection was never mentioned amongst this sexual élite who had no fears that even the oddest longing would not find a taker in this do-it-yourself market of sexual styles. The confidence was brash and alienating when sexual angst centres so strongly round fear of failure and loss. There was an assumption that the liberatory moment came at the point when sexual preference was defined, that to define was sufficient, to question not required:

> The workshop will attempt to open up the Pandora's Box of sexual styles, attitudes and roles banished from the Feminist Movement as 'politically incorrect'. [The convenors] propose that these styles should be examined and lived.[1]

The poles of the discussion were the extension of female choice as opposed to patriarchal male restriction:

> The ninth The Scholar and The Feminist conference will address women's sexual pleasure, choice, and autonomy, acknowledging that sexuality is simultaneously a domain of restriction, repression, and danger as well as a domain of exploration, pleasure and agency ... to speak only of pleasure and gratification ignores the patriarchal structure in which women act, yet to talk only of sexual violence and oppression ignores women's experience with sexual agency and choice.[2]

Women, in other words, have only to take power into their own hands; there are no subjective problems – of fear, inhibition; only objective ones – only the patriarchy prevents the indefinite expansion of women's pleasure and sexual power.

At first I felt inadequate at having to admit that I had none of these 'outlawed' desires, an admission akin to that of having never sniffed cocaine. To have questioned the centrality of incorrect sexual styles to the feminist project would have been worse than revealing oneself as inadequate; it would have been radically to question the terms in which others had defined themselves; would have been rude and threatening; not as uncool as sneezing *before* you had sniffed the coke, as Woody Allen did in *Annie Hall*, but ultimately worse, for you would have thereby defined yourself as the spoil-sport who refuses to play the game at all.

Clearly many women found the occasion profoundly challenging and exciting, just as many feminists had found the Sex Issue of *Heresies* to be saying things they wanted to hear.[3] To me that number of *Heresies* might as well have been the General Motors Catalogue (and I am just not interested in cars). But as I pondered my failure to respond with excitement to all this 'radical' sex I realized that romantic fantasy is another kind of turn on. It is a specifically women's turn-on, and has been catered for by the millions of pulp romances that are churned out year after year. That, perhaps, was *my* turn-on too. When I thought about it, my fantasies and real life desires (if they can be separated) were structured less around particular sexual acts than around a constellation of turn on feelings that had to do with star crossed or illicit love, with desires that were magical because forbidden. Those periods of my life that had on the surface appeared secure in the harmony of an established relationship had been riddled with secret longings, all the more compelling if they came to nothing. My private life itself had been seamed into levels of privacy, in which the intimacy of the couple was only an ante-chamber to the darker solitude of those romantic loves that could of course only either have foundered in the calm of coupledom or ended with the nausea that comes when unfulfilled desires go stale.

Such problems are banal. The contradiction between a constructive and purposeful life lived with the support of a trusted companion, and the longing for what Doris Lessing called the 'injection' of 'being in love' is an all too familiar theme. Yet it is one that has been to some extent banished by the avant-garde sexual discourses of the 1970s – discourses of which the Barnard Conference was one development. Romanticism has been in fact one of the great unspoken themes of the left-wing movements of the West during the decade now passed. Because it was not dealt with, it is returning in new forms and strange guises.

'Romantic' and 'romance' have long associations with literature and literary forms that involved tales about heroic figures. In medieval romance literature the adventures of heterosexual love, usually illicit, were cast as obstacles in the path of the hero, whose goal was the Grail or some sublime achievement or discovery. Even in the tales of courtly love, though love itself might be the goal, the hero subordinated himself to his 'mistress' and carried out feats of daring in order to prove his worthiness of her.

Romanticism as a movement was born with capitalism. But the nineteenth century hero is a more contradictory figure by far than his medieval forebear. Where the thirteenth century hero sought Truth and Enlightenment, the nineteenth century romantic seeks self-realization. The courtly knight's ideal of service to his liege lady might run in parallel to, or as a metaphor for a general ideal of the subordination of self to a higher purpose. In the nineteenth century service and subordination become contradictory. Once, the bravery of the hero was his bravery in pursuit of his Grail; now the heroism of the hero lies in his challenge to all restraint. He knows no boundaries, he can cross any frontier, and reach any goal. If, like Icarus, having mastered flight, he flies too near to the sun, that Satanic over-reaching is itself part of his glory. No matter what the frontier, to cross it becomes in itself the mark of the hero. The medieval hero had to be morally and spiritually fit to achieve his purpose – and Sir Lancelot was unfitted by reason of his adulterous love for Guinevere; now the hero's achievement of the frontier in itself makes him – retrospectively – fit to undertake the journey.

This modern romantic hero who will brook no denial becomes the rebel *par excellence*. The keynote of this romantic movement is a rejection of and rebellion against all that had gone before: the old order. The courtly knight venerated tradition; this new hero tramples on it. This makes him to some extent Satanic from the beginning. His hallmark is transgression.

Subordination to a mistress takes on a new and perverse tinge. The romantic hero is a free spirit. Why then should he voluntarily chain himself to a woman in the role of suppliant?

What is the lure of the impossible love? Here, with the suspicion of masochism, psychology enters the stage.

Yet also, how well suited was this new ideology of romanticism to the capitalistic spirit from which it appeared so radically divorced, so much in conflict. For central to both is the element of *risk*. In capitalism: 'the possibility of failure becomes the postulate of a moral excuse for profit'.[4] The successful entrepreneur is the man who dares to risk his capital – and his reputation – both in order to increase his own wealth and, or so they tell us, to increase the wealth of the nation and thus further the national good.

A similar task is present in romantic love. The lover declares his love as the gambler declares his hand, for both love and capitalism are forms of gambling. In so doing he throws himself to the winds of fortune blown by the caprice of the woman he adores. The daring of this risk acts as justification for every kind of irrational and exaggerated behaviour. Irrationalism, in fact, becomes the hallmark of this new form of romantic love. The medieval knight's love for his mistress was based on a just appreciation of her virtue; the new romantics are proud to claim that the love they express is but the figment of their own imagination, it is not even an over-valuation of the beloved; it is actually the creation of the lover himself, as Stendhal symbolized it in his famous metaphor:

> Leave a lover with his thoughts for twenty-four hours, and this is what will happen:
>
> At the salt mines of Salzburg, they throw a leafless wintry bough into one of the abandoned workings. Two or three months later they haul it out covered with a shining deposit of crystals. The smallest twig, no bigger than a tom-tit's claw, is studded with a galaxy of scintillating diamonds. The original branch is no longer recognizable.
>
> What I have called crystallization is a mental process which draws from everything that happens new proofs of the perfection of the loved one ...
>
> The crystallization about your mistress, that is to say her *beauty*, is nothing but the sum of the fulfilment of all the desires you have been able to formulate about her.[5]

This process, which Stendhal calls an 'ideology', is pure subjectivity. The existence of the women is but a catalyst for the imaginings and fantasies of the lover.

At the same time, the subordination and abnegation of love does become a form of punishment for a generosity that capitalist society will not countenance:

> The prohibition of love ... later on became all the more effective the more love as ideology had to perform its work of deception about the hatred of competitors. In the world of commercial exchange, he who gives over the measure is in the wrong; whereas the lover is always he who loves beyond measure. Whereas the sacrifice that he brings is glorified, jealous care is taken to ensure that the lover is not spared a sacrifice. Love itself is the very place where the lover is made to do wrong and punished for his wrong-doing.[6]

In the world of capitalism, romantic love becomes more important. Feeling has been banished from the rest of social life, where the economic principle of profit dominates more and more. All feeling has to be crammed into the erotic relationship, and since eroticism is in any case to a large extent taboo, love relationships between men and women become inflamed and swollen with a weight of significance too much for them to bear.

It may seem perverse to have concentrated on an examination of the meaning for men in the nineteenth century of romantic love when the feminist perspective, developed initially by Germaine Greer, has been that romantic love spells thralldom for *women*.[7] Germaine Greer described romantic love as a kind of false consciousness brought on by the reading of trashy novels (a very Victorian idea!) and pulp romances as a direct form of ideology created to secure women's subordination. But this is much too simple, one-sided and one dimensional. In the realm of feelings reciprocity does exist, and so does thralldom for both sexes. The reading of pulp romance may be 'escapist', yet is involved at some level with pleasure. It is wrong to see the whole of modern life as a prison for women with men as both guards and judges. The vision of male

masters and female slaves purveyed by Andrea Dworkin,
although strangely attractive to many feminists, is nothing
more than a mirror image of the pornography it claims to
attack.[8]

The feminist response both to romantic fiction and to
romantic love has been to dismiss it as a form of false
consciousness. 'It only leads to housework.' Yet to understand
romantic love as nothing but the bait in the trap of marriage
and domestic servitude is fatally to ignore the content in the
romantic myths of our own time or the nineteenth century.

Of course the magic of dominance and submission is written
into romantic tales just as much as it is written into
pornography; and romance is a sort of pornography of the
feelings, where emotions replace sexual parts, yet may be just
as fetishized. The themes of romance are compulsion and
denial. In romance, feelings are not freely entered into; they
are stronger than oneself; the lover draws one on yet ultimately
denies. The moment of final consummation *has* to be the end
of the story because as Freud pointed out sexual gratification
destroys the compulsion little by little. New forms of affection,
or indeed thralldom, may ensure, but these are different from
romantic longing.

After all, domestic life is designed to maximise security
(however much it may fail); while danger is the essence of
romantic love. The romantic hero (or heroine) is essentially
'unsuitable' – 'mad, bad and dangerous to know' in the
famous phrase Lady Caroline Lamb used to describe her lover
Byron. What could be more wonderful than that? And Byron's
own poems, like the 'gothic' novels of the period, often rely on
the theme of the abducted heroine, victim in the coils of a
tormented tormentor. The feminine version of this figure is the
Belle Dame Sans Merci, the fatal enchantress, Circe the witch.

Why do these fantasies have the power to compel? One way
of looking at it would be to say that the danger of romantic
love acts as a drug, a substitute, or a form of escapism from the
tedium of a routinized daily life under capitalism. The
assembly line worker, the shop assistant, the girl in the typing
pool, must have their dreams, since reality is so monotonous.
But even if we were to accept that explanation with its tidy fit

between fantasy and economy, it would not explain the content of the dreams. Why does the path to adventure lie through the tent of the Sheik?

Romance, like some forms of pornography, approximates to a kind of Grail legend in seeming to resemble the journey of the questing individual in search of enlightenment. For women particularly, so long at least as the 'taboo of virginity' is powerful, romantic passion can be felt to have a strongly transforming power. For a young woman the first night of passion acts as a chasm between her previous life and her life henceforth. In a long chapter of *The Second Sex* Simone de Beauvoir demonstrated with many examples from diaries, memoirs, autobiography and novels the importance and significance of this moment, even when the reality is sadly unlike the myth.[9]

Sex becomes the *rite de passage* and as such a kind of rebirth. This may go some way to explain its association – within the romantic tradition at least – with death.

Like so many other features of modern life romantic love could be seen as a secularization of spiritual impulses that once expressed themselves in mysticism, ritual and magic. We cannot return to former beliefs. But the insufficiency of nineteenth century scientism and hyper-rationalisation has led rather to secular irrationalism – of which the most extreme form is of course fascism. And fascism has a romanticism all its own.

We cannot return to 'spiritual values', certainly not of a religious kind, for there is much truth in the nineteenth century rationalist view, so forcefully expressed by both Freud and Marx, that organized religious belief is not only deluded, based on an illusion, but often reactionary in its contents and usually for that reason dangerous in its effects. The alternatives we have in our culture: astrology, encounter groups, compulsions of many kinds, are, nonetheless, hardly adequate substitutes. Our culture *is* spritually impoverished, and because of this we all have all sorts of emotional impulses and needs that lack real nourishment.

Twentieth century socialism and feminism – like their parent culture – have been marked and indeed deformed by the nineteenth century scientism that dismissed all such impulses as hiccups of the nervous system. For more than 100 years the dominant scientific belief has been that everything can be explained in terms of positivistic science, by laws similar to those that rule the natural world. Subjectivity becomes essentially unreal, and sexuality confined to the status of an appetite, at best a natural need, at worst an animal function.

For some feminists, especially in the nineteenth century but also today too, sex has been perceived as the bestial appetite of the male; love (often between women) or celibacy then become essentially higher states. Alternatively, and this is a more twentieth century view, sexuality is perceived as 'the truth' about human feeling and the self. Sexuality (not romantic passion) becomes the moment of ultimate self-expression, self fulfilment and release.[10]

These two attitudes are two sides of the same coin. Both see sex as functional and appetitional; the difference lies only in what should be done about it. The first view sees the satisfaction of the appetite as weakening and debilitating; the second on the contrary as essential to functioning and health. Both views are rationalistic.

The puritan tradition is rather different, since it attempts a fusion not only of the sexual impulse and love, but also of passion and companionship. The puritan marriage relationship, whether celebrated within the church or by D H Lawrence, represents romantic passion solidified into monogamy.

The socialist tradition has at different times embraced (if I may use that word) all these approaches. It has been scientific – for example, when the Bolsheviks hotly disputed whether love was just 'a glass of water'. It has also been puritanical. At times romanticism has been seen as merely a form of bourgeois degeneracy, while the way in which the puritan tradition romanticizes marriage itself has been ignored or not understood. And the way in which the socialist tradition has tended to harness the monogamous couple as a unit gloriously forwarding the revolution and working together for a higher purpose romanticizes not only the couple but revolution itself.

Freud was a great debunker of romantic love: 'Sexual over-estimation is the origin of the peculiar state of being in love, a state suggestive of a neurotic compulsion.'[11] Yet although he too approached it from the perspective of a nineteenth century scientist, an ultra-rationalist, in another way his attempts at explanation do at least acknowledge the power of this 'neurotic compulsion', even if they are imbued with pessimistic determinism.

For Freud sees desire as essentially unfulfillable, and indeed as compelling precisely because of the obstacles in its way:

> An obstacle is required in order to heighten libido: and where natural resistances to satisfaction have not been sufficient men have at all times erected conventional ones so as to be able to enjoy love.[12]

Since he perceives erotic love as rooted in the infant's love of its parental figures, which in turn grows out of the satisfaction of the baby's bodily needs (and ultimately the need for survival), he views the state of being in love as a development of narcissism. The individual in love abandons his narcissism, but seeks indirect satisfaction for it by projecting it onto the idealized love object. Thereby he in a sense re-appropriates it. And although the satisfaction of the erotic longing usually leads to its diminution, sexual thralldom may be perpetuated when the resistances that had to be overcome were very great.[13]

Adult love, for Freud, is always to some extent a re-enactment of the grandiose and unfulfillable aspirations of the infant. Romantic passion really is, therefore, a longing for the impossible. Like so much else in Freud it represents the wish to escape the confines of reality and return to a former state of pleasure and happiness untinged by compromise. Late in life, Freud realised that that former state of bliss was different for the boy than for the girl. Or rather it was the same: in that the infant of both sexes experienced the nurturance and narcissism of babyhood in relation to a woman, the mother; and out of this sameness of experience comes the later difference of sexual desire, constructed differently for the boy who may continue to love erotically a woman all his life – and indeed must do so – than for the girl who must transfer her eroticism to a new object of desire, the male, the father.

Implicitly it also depends on the repression of overt sexuality, or at least of many of the more 'perverse' sexual impulses. The intensity of the passion arises out of one or other 'taboo' that stands in the way of its satisfaction.

Such an idea is anathema to modern feminism, which has been based on the belief that female sexuality should be unleashed and should be no longer taboo, no longer repressed. As one woman wrote in a letter to *Spare Rib*:

> I believe the erotic springs from our roots as women, and is a life-giving, powerful force at the centre of every woman. Men hate/fear this strength, have denied its existence, and have taught us to fear it ourselves. It is this fear that is at the root of pornography.
>
> So I see the struggle to reclaim the erotic as a power in our lives as a fundamental attack on male sexuality and power. If we ignore or suppress it then we are once again fighting against ourselves because of the guilt and uncertainty that men have put into our heads.[14]

This is a Reichian rather than a Freudian view. It is a popular vision both amongst feminists and in our culture as a whole, of sexual energy. But some feminists have understood that this vision of sex as 'natural' and therefore as relatively unmarked by culture does not help us understand the ways in which culture and subjectivity do create a whole superstructure of gender on the flimsy foundations of biological sex.

The New Left also, coming out of the same political 'moment' of 1968 as feminism, took as central to its project the disruption of repressed sexuality. In many ways that politics has now played itself out, and the 1970s revealed its many weaknesses. We can no longer see sexuality as some privileged sort of energy, the unleashing of which has subversive, let alone revolutionary implications. The Marcusean flowering of sexuality in a non-repressive post-revolutionary society is itself a romantic vision, Utopian in its conjuring up of an earthly paradise.

The traditional left has often been accused, on the other hand, of ignoring and repressing sexuality just as much as bourgeois society. To the extent that this 'traditional left' has not taken seriously the problems of sexuality and gender as part of the politics of the personal it is to be criticized. At times, however, this failure is construed not simply as a gap or failing but as such a fatal flaw that it calls into question the socialist project as a whole, almost as if, because Marxist groups and parties have not grasped the full implications of sexism, the whole theory of surplus value falls and the concept of class struggle become irrelevant. Such criticisms are destructive and sectarian, often more to be distinguished for their anti-Marxism than for their good sense. To understand that power relations structure private life (to politicize the personal) does not – or at least should not – lead to the conclusion that not to address every aspect of personal life at every moment is to fall into some form of Stalinism.

In any case, as I wandered amongst the American feminists on Morningside Heights I began to have doubts. Is *everything* to do with sex automatically political? To what extent is sexuality ultimately amenable to political solutions? Are not some aspects of sexuality, like growth or the ageing process, a kind of bedrock of human experience around which politics develops but which are not, in themselves, inevitably political?

Amongst American feminists two themes of lesbian sexuality, sado-masochism and butch-femme relationships (sex role stereotyping and role playing within lesbianism) were the focus of much discussion at Barnard and in the Sex Issue of *Heresies*. These practices have been defended as forms of sexual 'outlawry'. In part this seems to be a reaction against the desexualization of lesbianism by some radical feminists. Adrienne Rich for example has written:

> I mean the term *lesbian continuum* to include a range ... of woman-identified experience; not simply the fact that a woman has had or consciously desired genital experience with another woman.[15]

In emphasizing 'politically unacceptable' lesbian eroticism, it seems as if some lesbians are tring to put the sex back into their identity, which, in 'political lesbianism' seems to them to have become sexless, and 'lesbianism' merely a synonym for feminism.[16]

The statement that lesbianism is *not* first and foremost about being a feminist or about rejecting men (which the dominant culture says it is) is an important one. The notion of 'sexual outlawry' has become a significant part of this assertion, this attempt to retrieve erotic sexuality between women from the amorphous euphemisms or insipidity of being merely in some global way 'woman identified'.

Yet here, in a seemingly unlikely quarter perhaps, we encounter romanticism once more. For the whole notion of outlawry is essentially romantic. Because homosexuality is no longer so wholly taboo, then a further frontier of the damned and the dangerous has had to be drawn.

(And of course the Romance of Revolution has nourished itself on the Outlaw too. If 'actually existing socialism' becomes bureaucratic and banal that is at least partly because the revolutionary quality of the revolutionary resides to some extent in his oppositional state. As an outlaw the romantic hero often represents the power of the powerless.)

Yet the lesbian sadomasochism of the 1980s in metropolitan America is trying to have it both ways. It relies on a structure of romantic fantasy, yet reduces romance to sexual games playing and dressing up, so that instead of speaking our subjectivity it is in danger of becoming just another part of the commodity culture. The fantasy is power, domination and even perhaps cruelty, but the practice is specially constructed to make it all safe, honest and in the open – the very negation of the dark fantasy.

Romantic passion represents a longing for that which has been lost. The high point of the operatic movement of love is loss. Madame Butterfly's famous aria, for example, recreates in a long drawn out sequence the moment of her lover's return. 'I see him coming,' she sings; she describes his boat lifting over the horizon – it docks – he disembarks – he is climbing the path to her house – at last he nears the door – she runs away and hides to prolong the delicious agony – he calls her name … and so on.

The astonishing thing about this celebration of reunited lovers – and the whole charge of the music – is that Captain Pinkerton is *never there at all*. This, the climactic moment of the whole opera, is a celebration of *absence*, of the gaping void left by romantic love.

Socialism, which is an optimistic creed, has necessarily had difficulty in dealing with these levels of subjectivity and has had no answer to the problem of what lies 'beyond the pleasure principle'. Feminism has approached problems of subjectivity and has had some success in the construction of theory, yet the theory has tended to produce a divorce from practical politics rather than drawing the two closer together. For example, the way in which feminists have used psychoanalytic theory to analyse sexual desire has had nothing to say about lesbianism[17] and in most cases has been unable to deal with the stark reality of rape and violence towards women in a way that expresses an appropriate degree of indignation or can mobilize women against abuse, without at the same time simply blaming 'men' and 'male power' or 'male sexuality' in the simplistic fashion of Andrea Dworkin and most other 'radical feminists'.

In confronting the romantic we seem to reach a parameter of the political. While feminists have been right to point to the role of sexuality in securing women's subordination, and while romanticsm can be seen as a part of the construction of ideologies of that subordination, this does not mean that the 'liberation' of women necessarily comes about by means of a direct 'liberation' of female sexuality, whatever that would mean. Nor does it meant that in unmasking ideologies we have destroyed or ever understood the romantic impulse. This is not a plea for the recuperation of the romantic and romanticism as somehow progressive, nor is it a reiteration of it as an ideology of control. It is simply an attempt to restate an unresolved problem: what is the relationship of politics to emotions? The feminist movement went too far in equating the two, so that at times anything a woman felt was automatically assumed to be politically correct. Because we have romantic feelings does not necessarily mean they are good or progressive; because our culture supports them does not mean they are automatically bad or reactionary. In pursuing the demon lover through the recesses of the psyche we shall not regenerate Marxism nor discover better forms of political practice. But we might understand subjectivity better, and learn more about the intermittance of human happiness. (And politics, after all, is supposed to be about happier lives.) So, in exploring romanticism, we may come to have less grandiose visions of what the political can accomplish, and cease to denounce all politics that does not promise us utopia.

References

1 Diary of a Conference on Sexuality; Diary of the Months the Galaxor and the Feminist Conference, New York, 1982.
2 Ibid.
3 *Heresies*, Number 12, Sexuality Issue, 1981. *Heresies* is an American feminist periodical. The Sexuality Issue confronted a number of problems both in defining sexuality and in challenging some of the latent assumptions and prejudices within feminism about how feminists 'should' express their sexuality; it had articles on 'butch-femme' relationships, sadomasochism, pornography, 'fag-hagging' (women who relate to homosexual men), celibacy and feminist erotica.
4 Theodor Adorno and Max Horkheimer, *The Dialectic of Englightenment,* London, 1972.
5 Stendhal, *Love*, Harmondsworth, 1975, pp.45-46.
6 Adorno and Horkheimer, op. cit.
7 Germaine Greer, *The Female Eunuch*, London, 1970.
8 Andrea Dworkin, *Pornography: Men Possessing Women*, London, 1981.
9 Simone de Beauvoir, *The Second Sex*, London, 1953, Part IV, Chapter III.
10 cf Michel Foucault, *The History of Sexuality: An Introduction*, London, 1979 and Jeffrey Weeks, *Sex, Politics and Society*, London, 1981.
11 Sigmund Freud, 'On Narcissism', *Collected Papers*, Volume IV, London, 1948.
12 Sigmund Freud, 'On the Universal Tendency to Debasement in the Sphere of Love', *Standard Edition*, Volume 11, London.
13 Sigmund Freud, 'Contributions to the Psychology of Love: The Taboo of Virginity', *Collected Papers*, Volume IV, London, 1948.
14 Letter in *Spare Rib*, Number 115.
15 Adrienne Rich, *Compulsory Heterosexuality and Lesbian Existence*, London, 1981, pp.20-21.

16 cf Wendy Clark, 'The Dyke, the Feminist and the Devil' in *Feminist Review* Number 11, 1982, pp. 30-40.

17 Janine Chasseguet Smirgel, *Female Sexuality: New Psychonanalytic Views*, Ann Arbor, 1970. Feminists sometimes use this book, which contains essays on lesbianism, which are, however, uninformed by feminism and treat lesbianism as a 'lesser of two evils' solution to maintain a precarious stability.

Angela Carter
Alison's Giggle

In the Miller's Tale of *The Canterbury Tales* by Geoffrey Chaucer, a young woman, who has just played a sexual practical joke on a young man whom she does not want, emits a satisfied giggle. We know Alison giggles rather than bursts out laughing, because Chaucer tells us that she does so: 'Tehee! quod she.' She giggles; and returns to bed with a more attractive partner. Her husband, meanwhile, has strung himself up in a tub under the rafters, awaiting the arrival of the Flood, which his wife and her lover has convinced him is imminent so that he will vacate his bed and leave it to them. (Alison's husband believes the tub will make an excellent improvised boat and proposes to launch it at the first sign of the inundation by cutting the ropes which attach it to the roof.)

Alison's giggle is not a sound which is heard very often in literature, although, in life, it can be heard every time a young girl successfully humiliates a would-be admirer. (My mother taught me to say this to young men in dance halls who wanted to buy me gin and orange even though they had spots: 'Does your mother know you're out?' Off they would squelch, abashed, on their two-inch thick crêpe soles. And we girls would giggle.) Perhaps, given the traditional male narrator in literature, the sound is so rarely heard just because it expresses the innocent glee with which women humiliate men in the only way available to them, through a frontal attack on male pride. To reproduce this giggle, a man must identify with a woman rather than with another man and perceive some aspects of male desire as foolish. Indeed, in a sense, perceive the idea of the supremacy of male desire as foolish.

Admittedly, Chaucer, through the mouth of the Miller whom he has invented to tell this tale, is careful to present Alison's failed suitor, Absolon, the parish clerk, as a ninny; that makes it easier for them both to take Alison's point of view. All the same, Absolon, looked at objectively, is no more of a ninny than Don Jose in *Carmen*, who also attempts to thrust his attentions on a woman who is no longer interested. But Prosper Merimée saw nothing foolish about *his* hero. And, even if he *is* a ninny, Absolon is so roundly humiliated – Alison tricks him into kissing her backside, rather than her mouth – most men would think she'd gone too far. But, in the tale, Absolon's vengeance goes badly wrong and misses Alison altogether; and, more significantly, Alison is not censured by her creator for asserting a woman's right to humiliate in however light-hearted and girlish a fashion.

Alison's giggle sets up a series of echoes disturbing our preconceptions whilst echoing our experience. If male narrators, in general, cannot bear to hear it, the female narrator, increasingly frequent over the last two hundred years, especially in those forms of the novel that purport to give an exact transcription of everyday life and so ought to tally better with our experience than medieval poetry does, have also tended to omit both the giggle and the kind of sexual circumstance that best provokes it.

Hard to imagine Jane Austen's Elizabeth Bennett playing a sexual practical joke on the curate in *Pride and Prejudice* who so richly deserves it, and not only because Jane Austen's genteel scenario, centuries away from that of the 'fabliau' of the middle ages, does not allow to take place the kind of events in the course of which Mr Collins might, literally, kiss Elizabeth's arse. (Indeed, linguistically, Elizabeth is not in possession of an arse.) And, apart from these limitations, Jane Austen arrives in history at that curious time when women, as a fiction reading as well as a fiction writing class, were supposed to affect ignorance of just exactly what it was Alison was up to in bed with her Nicholas when she was interrupted by the unwelcome serenade of the parish clerk.

Whether a *female* narrator of Chaucer's period would have felt the Chaucerian freedom of diction and situation is moot. The female narrators whom Chaucer invents himself are

perfectly decorous in diction, although the Wyf of Bath's tale is
not particularly decorous in content and her soliloquies on
life, love and the management of husbands have badly upset
centuries of male commentators. The Wyf of Bath is, however,
a fictional invention, and her self-determined sexual appetites
('I folwed ay myn inclinacioun,' she says) and her robust
speech belong to the sexual stereotype of the middle-aged
woman, who may speak as she pleases since the sexual threat
she poses has been removed by the menopause. She is the same
kind of fictional person as the nurse in Shakespeare's *Romeo and
Juliet*; and as Mae West. Situation complicated, here, by the
fact that Mae West was both a fictional invention, a woman
who re-invented herself in terms of the movies she wrote and
starred in, and also a perfectly real woman who, it would seem,
often behaved and spoke like the fictional Mae West.
Stereotypes only become stereotypes, after all because they
correspond to certain kinds of real behaviour. It is possible to
surmise, therefore, that there were sufficient middle-aged
women rich enough and tough enough to behave not unlike
the Wyf of Bath in England in the fourteenth century, which is,
in many ways, a daunting thought.

Such a woman, with a perfectly good trade of her own (the
Wyf of Bath was a famous weaver of cloth) and a very active
sexual and emotional life, would scarcely have had the time to
write poetry, nor, one imagines, would she have seen the point
of the activity. And she may not have known how to read and
write too well (although she could certainly count.) Marie de
France, the twelfth century poetess (called 'de France' because
she was a Frenchwoman who lived in England) composed
infinitely elegant poetic tales of impeccably courtly love,
befitting a person with a nice mind and, presumably, a private
income. However, since women certainly contributed to the
anonymous body of traditional lyric which survives in
manuscript from the medieval period, and survives in other
forms in folk songs collected in the nineteenth century, and
which is often very rude indeed, it is possible that *illiterate*
women may have had a freedom of creative expression, and
the opportunity to do so, denied to those of higher rank and
accomplishment.

Whether women could, if the possibility had been widely

available, have written in a 'Chaucerian' manner in Chaucer's time is an unanswerable question; but we know that medieval women, of whatever class, were not supposed to be shocked by Chaucer because *The Canterbury Tales* was intended for a mixed sex audience. There are two women on the pilgrimage itself, one the Wyf of Bath and the other a nun, who listen and comment upon a collection of stories many of which, by Jane Austen's time, were not considered suitable for women at all, at all. When the Miller sums up his tale in the phrase, 'Thus swyved was the carpenterys wife' ('That's how the carpenter's wife got herself fucked'), it may be assumed that not only the male pilgrims and the Wyf of Bath but also the nun knew what 'to swyve' meant and did not think it reprehensible or unusual activity between consenting adults.

The representations of women in English literature by male narrators (and we can assume a dominant male narrator until the mid-eighteenth century) are, however much determined by contemporary notions of the position of women, based on the assumption that men and women share an equal knowledge of the basic facts of sexual experience up until, curiously enough, that very time in the eighteenth century when women in significant numbers take up their pens and write. The poet, the writer of fiction and the dramatist always write in the context of the assumed knowledge of the listener, the reader, the spectator; when, for whatever reasons, there comes about a time when rather more than half the audience for any given literary production is presumed to be in ignorance of the basic facts of the continuation of the human race. Then a whole group of literary productions becomes 'unsuitable for women', especially those in which women *are* shown as knowledgable and active sexual beings. (Witness the wrath the nineteenth century inflicted on Restoration comedy and the way the female dramatist, Mrs Aphra Behn, became unmentionable, due to her 'indecent' wit.)

It is not a naive question, that of whether Jane Austen, a provincial maiden lady, was herself precisely aware of the actual mechanics of sexual intercourse. It is reasonable to assume, from the degree of sexual tension between her female and male characters, that, even if she were unfamiliar with the practice, she was conversant with the theory, to some degree. The twanging eroticism of Austen's novels may even owe some of its power to the taboo upon pre-marital or extra-marital sexual intercourse and upon discussion of these things in any but the broadest terms. Yet the conventions of her time and class, conventions of both fiction and of actual behaviour, force her to deny to her heroines the practical use of the sexual allure with which she so abundantly equips them – assuming, that is, she did indeed know just what such use would mean.

The sexuality of Austen's heroines exists as a potential; as a potential, it is fully utilised as lure and bait. But her narratives ceased abruptly with the marriages of the heroines, although this is the point at which, for the British bourgeoisie of the late eighteenth century, a woman's life actually begins. That is, her *real* life, as mistress of a house and as a being-in-the-world; all this is symbolised by marriage as the beginning of a woman's sexual life.

Austen shares this cut-off point in her heroine's stories both with the nameless authors of fairy tales and with most writers of fiction primarily intended for a female market in her own day and in ours. Her heroines remain electric virgins, charged with a power of which they know the value – indeed, perhaps they over-value it – just as long as it remains within their own control. But, as regards that power in the context of a marriage, when the woman herself is no longer in complete control of it – for Austen, and, perhaps, for many women, this remains unquantifiable, and not only if they remain unmarried. Austen ends her heroines' stories at the moment when the virgin is about to die as a virgin, and be born again as – and, you see, there is no word for it. No word for a 'respectable' woman as a heterosexual being except 'wife,' that is, by definition, a contingent being.

If both words, 'virgin' and 'wife', define a woman by her sexual status, 'virgin' describes a condition-in-itself, while the word 'wife' implies the existence of a husband, just as the word 'prostitute' implies the existence of a client.

Even so, the conventionalised 'happy ending' of the wedding in fiction by and for women may signify not so much the woman's resignation of her status as autonomous individual, a

status that might be at best problematic in a society with little
available space for anybody's autonomy, but the woman's
acquisition of a licence to legitimately explore her own sexuality
in relation to a man, as well as aquiring part shares in her
husband's public status and wealth, and inheriting all the
folklore of sex and reproduction that is passed from
generation to generation of married women. For a woman, to
marry, in fiction, is to grow up; all the same, there is
something rather honourable about the simple reluctance of
fiction by and for women to accommodate itself to that kind of
maturity. The narratives stop short at the altar, as if they
cannot bear to go on. As if to travel hopefully, the chase, the
courtship, the acceptance or rejection of suitors, were better
than to arrive at this ambivalent destination. All such fictional
narratives of women that end in marriage could just as well
end with a death, because marriage means the death of the
virgin, that is, the termination of her narrative as an individual,
however hedged about with prohibitions that individualism
might be.

Alison, the carpenter's wife, is brusquely defined by her
sexual status in a perfectly straightforward way. Since she is a
wife, we know she is not a virgin and also that her sexuality
belongs to somebody else. Further, she carries her husband's
social status around with her like a badge. Artisan class. (The
Wyf of Bath, by the way, is simply a woman from the city of
that name; she's had too many husbands to be easily defined
by the status of one of them and has, besides, a perfectly good
status of her own. Alison's story does not end with marriage; she
is married before her story begins and the plot quickens when
she becomes the focus of male extra-marital desire. Alison is a
contingent being in every way. We are not even given a hint of
her former history as a virgin; whether or not she, like the Wyf
of Bath, had 'other company in youth' is a mystery. But
marriage has not robbed her of the ability to keep her hands
on the reins of her own life; she can grab back control of her
sexuality and compensate herself thereby for some, at least, of
the more unpleasant consequences of marriage to a silly old
man.

George Eliot's *Middlemarch*, unlike the novels of Jane

Austen, begins with the marriage of its heroine, a marriage the
success of which is indicated by the scene in which we find
Dorothea Casaubon, on her honeymoon, weeping in a
cemetery. The tears of Dorothea come from a different world,
a different kind of experience and an utterly different narrator
than the giggle of Alison. Eliot is a woman. Chaucer is a man.
The two fictional women demonstrate the change in fiction in
the intervening five hundred years: Dorothea, clever, sensitive,
middle-class, aspiring towards she knows not what, is an
inhabitant of the fully three-dimensional Victorian novel with
its project of transmitting the whole of human life irradiated
by a vision of a transcendent morality. If that, too, was
Chaucer's project in *The Canterbury Tales*, he went about it in a
different way, and his Alison is an inhabitant of the
shadowless, two-dimensional world of medieval fabliau, the
eighteen year old wife of an artisan whose class has
disappeared from bourgeois fiction by George Eliot's day,
except as picturesque extras mumbling proverbs and old saws
in dialect. Alison is coltish and wild, slim as a weasel, with a
'likerous ye,' (a lecherous eye). She is described as an object of
desire, not from the inside. She is compared to a young pear
tree, a colt, a calf, a flower; all in all, the typical young girl of
male imagination. Yet, when she giggles, that 'Tehee! quod
she' comes rippling across the centuries, giving that entirely
spurious sense which only the greatest art gives us, that the
past, in all its unimaginable difference from our lives, can
nevertheless shiver, fall apart and reveal human beings who,
for all they believe the sun went round the earth, lived on the
same terms with themselves that we do and made the same
kind of compromises with circumstances.

Dorothea's dilemma, marriage to a man she finds sexually
odious and from which there is no way out except his death, is
presented by George Eliot as a paradigmatic moral dilemma
which has nothing to do with Dorothea's sexuality, nor with
desire nor with pleasure – least of all, with pleasure. It is just
possible to imagine Jane Austen, had she been born, not a
vicar's daughter in the Home Counties but into that world of
the amoral Regency aristocracy which scared her so much (see
her treatment of the Crawfords in *Mansfield Park*) thoroughly

endorsing Alison's strategy for the perpetuation of pleasure after marraige – that is, infidelity and the use of her sex as a weapon. Jane Austen's heroines have a glittering confidence in their own allure, even if it is always allure and never the lineaments of gratified desire. Fifty years later, Eliot, a writer of infinitely greater intellectual resources than Austen, effectively begged the entire question of the sexual nature of the heroine of her finest novel by presenting it in such an oblique way that Dorothea seems almost asexual and is constantly assimilated to unsexed female images of saints.

Yet Dorothea weeps on her honeymoon; and it is her husband Casaubon's attempt to regulate her actual sexual behaviour – according to his will, her inheritance depends on her *not* marrying the young, toothsome Will Ladislaw – that finally causes her to rebel. Casaubon, in his senile jealousy, noticed something that F.R. Leavis, in his commentary on the novel, did not, something Eliot veiled in sentimentality but did not entirely obscure – that Dorothea, even if she does look like a cinquecento madonna, is subject to the ancient sexual law of 'like unto like' upon which the Miller's tale is based. Dorothea wants to sleep with Ladislaw because he is young and handsome, and so is she. In their social context, to 'sleep with' means to marry. So marry they must and, in order tactfully to indicate that there are no tears on *this* honeymoon, Dorothea's story ends, not with the marriage, but with the birth of her child.

What is odd about all this discretion is that George Eliot herself led a sexual and emotional life that would have been considered unusually rich and full even by liberal late twentieth century standards, and was perfectly well aware that marriage, in reality, is neither an end nor a beginning but only a legislative change, and also that one does not need to marry men in order to sleep with them. Within the bounds of the conventions of her time, Eliot succeeds in writing about sexual relationships as they are, not as they should be, to a quite remarkable degree; her grasp of emotional logic is as straightforward as Chaucer's was. All the same, those tears of Dorothea in the Italian cemetery are a kind of code, a code which, at that period, only married women, i.e. non-virgins, were supposed to understand, although those tears tell us more, perhaps, than we might wish to know about Casaubon as a husband, and fill in many of the gaps in the idealised characterisation of Dorothea herself. Those tears, in fact, prepare the reader for her eventual remarriage; they tell us that Dorothea is a sexual being and her protracted intellectual disillusionment with her husband has started off from an equally unforgiveable sexual disappointment.

I suspect George Eliot would have been glad to have been able to describe the nature of that disappointment in more detail, if not in the self-same language used by Chaucer's Miller. However, it was not permissible for her to do more than hint; and, unsatisfactory and destructive as her marriage is, once Dorothea is married she is condemned to weep over her frustration without her inventor being able to tell us, in so many words, that this is what ails her. Both Dorothea and her inventor must present this aspect of the failure of the marriage between Dorothea and Casaubon as if it were of peripheral significance to Dorothea.

However, such is Eliot's respect for, and partial idealisation of the beautiful and saintly woman she has invented that, as well as convention and acceptability, a resistance to acknowledging Dorothea's sexuality in a more explicit way on Eliot's own part prevents *this* plot quickening at the notion of extra-marital intercourse. Small town gossip would have singled out the friendship between Dorothea and the handsome Dr Lydgate as almost certain to blossom into the right, true end of two unsatisfactory marriages. Eliot hints at this as a might-have-been; a union that would have redeemed Lydgate from the besetting sin of his own vulgarity, if – even without the complicating factor of their two spouses – Dorothea had shown the least sign of being attracted to a 'manly' Englishman of Lydgate's type. Since Dorothea gladly throws up her inheritance in order to marry an effete, curly-headed Slav, it would seem that Lydgate was the last kind of man she'd find attractive. By the end of the novel, marriage has taught Dorothea one important lesson – now she knows just what and whom she wants, and takes it the moment it is offered her. She wants, in fact, the kind of pretty, malleable man strong women very often want. (It is odd how many people find this aspect of the novel unsatisfactory, or unlikely.)

But all this is dealt with in such a discreet way that Eliot seems almost to be censoring herself. Eliot is certainly capable of presenting women who *are* deeply aware of their sexual being; in the same novel, Lydgate's wife, Rosamund, is perfectly aware, and is presented by Eliot as a poisonous, manipulative bitch.

The sexual relations between the Lydgates are left, of course, unstressed, although they produce children in due order so we know the marriage has been consummated. If there is a suggestion Rosamond is frigid, this is depicted as no more than an aspect of her selfishness; Lydgate can't possibly have anything to do with it.

Eliot castigates Lydgate for his foolishness in thoughtlessly marrying a pretty girl in the same way as he might have acquired an attractive piece of bric-à-bric, but the piece of bric-à-bric in question is condemned for no more than – being a piece of bric-à-brac. (Which is just how Rosamund tends to think of herself; as a precious ornament for a home, a fine possession for a man. This is a bad way for a woman to be in, but Eliot spares her no pity.) George Eliot neither likes nor approves of Rosamund and treats her touching provincial aspirations to material comfort, to social position, to respect, with contempt. But the relish with which she describes Rosamund's long-term corrosion of Lydgate's self-satisfaction has something self-contradictory about it. Reprehensible as Rosamund might be, her campaign of attrition against her husband may be read as the prototype of the revenge of any disappointed wife. She does to Lydgate what Dorothea, were Dorothea not such a saintly human being, might have felt perfectly justified in doing to Casaubon. (And, of course, we know with hindsight that Lydgate's medical research into the origins of typhoid will, on the evidence the novel gives us of its nature, lead him up just the same blind alley as Casaubon's theological research has led *him* – not that Eliot could have known that, of course.)

But Eliot – and this is a recurring phenomenon with the

female narrator – simply can't bear to put her beloved Dorothea in a bad light. Dorothea is not allowed to exhibit the least resentment. She must be the type of the 'Patient Griselda', who suffers in silence the tyranny of an appalling husband, gaining treasure in heaven thereby. 'Patient Griselda', idealisation of one type of medieval wife as Alison is the crystallisation of a more down-to-earth variety. Rosamund Ludgate, with far more of the Alison in her make-up than the Griselda, is offered to us as a 'bad woman', in contrast to Dorothea's 'good woman'. Rosamund is judged in the text by her narrator for her embittered attitude to her husband and found wanting; Dorothea is celebrated for concealing her bitterness. Yet both suffer the same affliction, which was Alison's affliction, too; all are married to men whom they do not, to use a shorthand phrase, love.

The nineteenth century bourgeois novel is in the business of making judgements. The medieval fabliau was not. Chaucer, and the Miller, suspend judgement on everyone. Yet it's noticeable that Absolon, Nicholas and even the carpenter – all the men in the story, in fact, suffer some kind of hurt, either of the feelings or the body. Absolon is tricked into kissing Alison's backside; intent on revenge, he returns with a red hot iron bar and asks for another kiss. However, Alison's lover, Nicholas, decides it would be fun if *he* were to stick his backside out of the window, this time, and so it is Nicholas, not Alison, who is branded on the buttock. When Nicholas cries out for water to cool his smart, the carpenter believes the Flood must have at last arrived, cuts the rope keeping his tub hanging in the rafters, and falls to the floor, breaking an arm. Only Alison, the adulterous wife and heartless humiliator of men, ends the story in as fresh, lively and 'likerous' a way as she began it.

Unjudged, perhaps, because not deemed responsible for her own actions, being so young, so coltish, so female? When the miller concludes: 'Thus swyved was this carpenterys wife' the use of the passive mood is striking. But at least Alison managed to get herself fucked by the man of her choice, to her own satisfaction and with no loss of either her own self-respect or the respect of her male creator, which is more than a girl like her will be able to do again, in fiction, for almost more than half a millenium.

Very well. Alison is a characater in an extended joke, not in a three-decker novel, even if that extended joke forms part of a long novel in the form of a poem that describes Chaucer's world and preoccupations as fully as *Middlemarch* does George Eliot's. But when she giggles, after Absolon has kissed her bum in error, she turns into a person who is literally uncontainable within the limitations of the kind of novel Eliot wrote and even, perhaps, uncontainable within Eliot's ability to imagine.

Alison will have one or two naughty sisters in other medieval fabliaus, a handful of rather more vicious great-great-granddaughters in Restoration comedy, but nobody in literature quite like her, with her light heart and her guiltlessness, until Colette summoned up her own girlhood in order to invent Claudine, nearly six hundred years later. And even Colette would have been unable to express, with such limpid simplicity, what it is that Nicholas does to Alison, could not have written down the Burgundian dialect equivalent of 'to swyve' and assumed all her readers would know what she meant without a gloss, would have been able to count on her readers not needing to have the activity spelled out blow by blow or euphemistically mystified.

In fact, Chaucer *does* expand a little on the swyving. He tacitly assumes his audience is perfectly familiar with the organs involved and so on, an assumption it might be gross to make even today, so he has no need to describe thrusting pistons or yielding walls or anything like that. He sums up the encounter thus:

> And thus lith Alison and Nicholas
> In bisynesse of myrthe and of solas.

Laughter and consolation. Nothing Lawrentian or metaphysical about *this* coupling; simply, it is as much as any sane person can hope for from sex and more, perhaps, than Alison deserves.

Then the serenader interrupts them. Alison humiliates him and giggles. If Colette could have entertained the possibility of that giggle, the female narrators who followed her in the latter part of the twentieth century would find it difficult to let their heroines get away with it. Anna, in *The Golden Notebook*; the lugubrious heroine of Marilyn French's *The Women's Room*; the moonstruck demi-vierges of Jean Rhys – to none of them, is adultery less than an existential challenge, while sexuality, either male or female, is no laughing matter and good women do not behave badly to men but gain treasure in heaven by letting men behave badly to them.

These heroines must be blameless, or else they cannot be heroines. They are recycled Patient Griseldas, tyrannised, not by one man as Griselda was, but by the entire sex, and now idealised by women themselves, rather than by men. The very question of sexual pleasure is hedged around with ambiguities and the desire to please is often mistaken for the desire for pleasure. When these heroines go to bed with their men, 'myrthe and solas' are the last things on their minds, which is just as well, since these things are rarely on offer.

There is a moving passage by Theodor Adorno, in *Minima Moralia*:

> Society constantly casts woman's self-abandon back into the sacrificial situation from which it freed her. No man, cajoling some poor girl to go with him, can mistake, unless he be wholly insensitive, the faint moment of rightness in her resistance, the only prerogative left by patriarchal society to woman, who, once persuaded, after the brief triumph of refusal, must immediately pay the bill.

Well, yes. Frigidity in the Victorian married woman, the headaches, the neurasthenia, the fabled vague ill-health that drove her husband into the arms of whores, may be seen as no more than a strategy of self-preservation, in the light of the maternal mortality statistics. (In the light of the ravages childbrith often inflicted upon women before the introduction of antisepsis and modern surgery, the lingering malaise of the married woman may, of course, have been genuine, protracted ill-health.) The nature of sexual repression in a society where heterosexual activity usually results in pregnancy and pregnancy may result in death is quite different from that of sexual repression in a society where birth control is freely available and childbirth is not feared, although, as Adorno implies, the ghosts of the old pain may not be so easily excorcised as all that.

Alison, unrepressed, giggles in the medieval fabliau, creation – however sympathetic – of a male narrator (and Chaucer is as sympathetic a male narrator as one will find in English literature, himself.) She and Chaucer live in a pre-bourgeois world, where women, as women, have somewhat more autonomy as workers and as beings-in-the-world than they will have by the time the novel, the bourgeois form of literature *par excellence*, is established. When this form becomes established, it becomes largely dominated by women themselves, as both readers and writers of fiction, and there seems to arise a conspiracy to deny women access through fiction to certain aspects of real life which are deemed unsuitable for them largely because they are concerned with sexual practice. There is some logic at work, here, a logic of repression related to the price of experience which is to do not with submission to the notion of the supremacy of male desire but an evasion of that presumed supremacy.

It should be noted that Alison seems untroubled by the idea of fertility. Perhaps, like the Wyf of Bath, she is fully aware of the 'remedies of love' (by which Chaucer presumably means abortificants); or, more likely, Chaucer temporarily forgot that sex often leads to babies. This is the characteristic sign of the male narrator everywhere in fiction. Either their mothers never told them, or the connection slipped their minds.

At the end of Colette's novel, *Ripening Seed*, the boy looks up at the window in which the girl whom he has just deflowered greets the morning with a song.

> From the window came a faint, happy little tune that passed over his head. Nor did the thought strike him that in a few weeks' time the child who was singing might well be standing in tears, doomed and frantic, at the same window.

The thought strikes Colette, of course; but it rarely strikes the male narrator. Phil continues meditating on how little the encounter has meant to his Vinca:

> A little pain, a little pleasure … That's all I shall have given her, that and nothing else … nothing …

So the novel ends, on a note of the bitterest irony; it is obvious from this that Colette intends the reader to understand that Vinca *has* conceived, and the seaside idyll of the teenage lovers is going to end very badly indeed. The connection between sex and reproduction does not slip a woman's mind so easily.

It is almost a cliché of orally transmitted poetry, that is, folk song, that one unprotected act of intercourse will lead inevitably to pregnancy; the pleasure principle remains undivorced from the reproductive function. Since performance of traditional song is fairly evenly divided between women and men, and the anonymous material is kept alive and often considerably altered in performance, it is fair to assume that women not only shape the songs they sing but invented some of them, long ago, in the first place.

> When I wore my apron low
> He followed me through frost and snow.
> Now I wear it to my chin
> He passes by and says nothing.

Although always found in the song called *Died for Love*, this is a 'floating' verse, that may be used at appropriate moments in all manner of different versions of different songs. Sex; pregnancy; desertion. That is a woman's life.

> I wish my baby little were born
> And smiling on its nurse's knee,
> And I myself were dead and gone
> For a maid again I'll never be.

Such songs were, no doubt, intended to help proscribe extra-marital sexual activity on the part of young village girls. Whether they had any effect on illegitimacy rates is now unguessable. However, the study of the representations of women in unofficial culture, in orally transmitted songs and stories, even in bar-room anecdotes, may prove a fruitful method of entry into the lived reality of the past. So may research into those forms of fiction that pre-date the bourgeois novel, in which the giggle of Alison, however disingenuous, suggests the possibility that, at some time in the past, a male narrator has been able to laugh at the pretensions of his own sex and therefore it is possible this may happen, again, in the future.

Michèle Roberts

judith and delilah and me

judith and delilah and me

when holofernes slept
then it was
that judith slew him
with his own sword
by her hand

when samson slept
then it was
that his strength left him
his own hair
by delilah's hand

before you sleep
I shall come before you, wet
and naked utterly, our
own bodies shall be
our pavilion you shall not
need to wound me
to escape
then
o fearful lion of judah
see
I shall take your sword
into my mouth I
shall lay my head
inside your mouth
samson carrying gates is lonely

lay your hands upon
my gates, grasp
my hair, bury
your sword, your fingernails
clotted with sweet wax
taste
the honeycomb
between my lion's jaws

judith returned home
married and bore six sons
became perhaps
an intolerable shrew
delilah at sixty
still has to
dance for a living

Klevshaven (Norwegian for 'Cleft haven')

this is a different country
the first night I was here

I was dry before I came
your lips parted to show me water
a spine of fur and molten sun
you called me across oceans
come to klevshaven

your house soaks me in sun, waking in
your bed at the heart of a marigold
your walls are white
I blink against them, lizard
in your hall's noonday

men and women built this landscape
bulldozers and lunchpails, gardens and funerals
the sun and aeroplanes twist above the river
when the sun goes down I smell your darkness

I wanted to slide further into you, klevshaven
and to suck your forest and hear your waters
crash in our silence, and to show you
the delicate mosses that grow there

my woman friend of ten years standing
those ten minutes when I lay beside you
were crammed with the riches of a life

there can be no rest
we have often parted before
we know we shall always
visit again
you stared across the mountain ridges of my hands
it is better to sleep now
my house accepts you in a different way

the rocks keep cropping up, boulders
piling in layers along the road
push at our talk of books and food
indefatigably monstrous, yet
their insides whorled as simply as sweets

I will suck them to swallow them down again
at night they are fluorescent and make me sick
each night the mountains swallow your sun
and my black sun
burns at noon in a snarl of gulls
to jag my flesh with my flesh

the woman in me is huge now
you are too close to see her perhaps
her pines scratch you instead
she rolls over carefully, her thighs
laid about the river, awaiting
her work, the explosion
to whorl her insides as simply as sweets

the attic is mine now, here
we gossip, our mothers' ghosts
their photographs and account books
recipes, patchwork
sobs and gestures
boil behind that door

nothing has changed
you said, you see?

you who are wise you know
plenty gone mad in flowered aprons
the screams in aspic and desire
bleached out on Monday
you who are wise you know
no herb will heal me

when I am from you

I shall not be dead, the fishbone
child who had choked me
swims on my words now
a woman
is fighting
not to be mermaid
calling you softly, klevshaven
klevshaven, klevshaven, women
have landscapes to build, men and women
have landscapes to build, to build

I am abroad in a strange land

I am abroad
in a strange land
loving a man again

I thought: this
is the capable man, broad
bones and a frame for
lifting; he knows
words and
winds, combs seas, views far
where the marsh sags
where the stream gobbles
the forest's hem
he will join hands
to make me a path across

I thought: I'll be the gentle field
waving with grass and smells
where he lies down, I'll be
his summer, his
scarlet poppy drug to
soothe him, he will suck
my silk, my wiry stem

it grows dark
now: the winter afternoon
smears light with mud
the sea dashes against a fragile wall
the forest's gone, grey into grey
the marsh sedge waves and sighs
a single heavy mass
alive with goblins
shrieks of sudden pits
the track through fear
too narrow for my single eye to thread
he's gone, he's lost
and therefore I am also gone

he loses me, he flails
a broken windmill in the sky
he names
me as the storm, me
as the grabbing marsh;
I shake, I hide, I name
him as the hunter, he
shoots my violent woods
my knocking sea

when we search for one another
winds muffle our words
we must call
loud, and hard
our feet inch
the chaotic earth

'Women's entry into culture is experienced as lack'

he wishes he were a
one of those able to
dance and shake
breasts and belly and hips
loose, a
not-himself, nothing-but

he wishes they did not have a
hiding from it in his bed stillness
he bruises easily
they will suck the blood
from their own   afterwards
alone

he wishes he were still a little boy
so that he did not have to face them
telling him he is an oppressor
he needs them to scold him
darling oppressor

if he were a
he could join the   movement
but at least his   friends
are always   who struggle
he has nothing to do but
help them out of
silence he has
nothing else to do
with   oppression
nothing else
nothing

he wishes they had a   too
so they could all just be friends

memories of trees

our confusion, to make men sound like gods:
unnatural woman, you are a tree
fixated, lost, with a deep gash
to be rained upon, rubbed up against
hidden in, struck down
sold, and burnt, your ashes
worthless

I plead, I can twist like metaphor
I approximate, I sway kneedeep
in ferns, I am cultivated, lovely
my bark is a thick plait

I rear myself near a woman lover
we are the hedges around farms
the milking-stool, the cradle
we furnish ships, and boxes
brooms, coffins, desks, and paper
we are your floors, your windows
our roots nourish us, twinned
labyrinthine memories, between us
passages, and gaps, and halts
the darkness wet beneath
the perplexed canopy of our hair

my father carves his name
on each in the plantation
clears our flowers, strips us
in a single word
I have stooped for years
I have smiled around him
now, when I fall upon him
crushing, still
he protests
you are my tree, only a tree

I too have words now, I have words

I am a woman in the city, I transform
nature, I survive
tempests; but my dreams
flower with him

the forest is long ago, is
deep coal
now
I pace the labyrinth
following the gold plait, thick, and knotted
when I find her, I am not only
heroine, but also
minotaur, she too

memories of trees
who never suffered pain
or yelled
or wept
or went away

punkrock; and Cocksparrow sings

I didn't expect it
(I like to know
what will happen, control it)
times have been hard, we were tired
(no you never get what you
want so don't
ask; if you are good, in fifty years' time
the revolution will give you
a book of instructions)

we went out dancing
in darkness, in glitter
an anniversary of sorts:
two women
six months of hard loving
hot little communion
with ninety others, your hands
root me, swaying in stars
your face, brighter than neon
I am sixteen as never then, fascinated
by sweat and satin and beer, the band
raucous, young boys on the dole
touching and innocent, yelling
mother, we are *so* bad; please
take us home
they hate the audience which
consumes them, their rage, their despair
I confront them, brazen
belonging: my hand in yours

back home to bed
you touched me gently: this could be
your benefit night
suddenly
you lay there laughing, your hand
leaping at me, come on
woman, come on; I flew

up and down
twice, and I came, it was simple
as that, I was amazed
and delighted, so proud
of myself, I didn't expect it
such prodigal
opening, such ease, and such
celebration

my bit of power
you never sang of, Cocksparrow
I compete with you still
last night I tried to forget
our separation, our
loneliness

unscientific

morning : he curls in bed, a dark
red bean sunk deep in under
a compost of
dreams and eiderdown

all night we are pits of sleep
twin beans, joined
in our cottony pod, skin
curved on skin

sun splits the curtains' case
clocks crack the warm earth
now I await
our green pushes
our scarlet flowers

Michèle Roberts

Jon Cook

Notes on History, Politics and Sexuality

'Things flow about so here!' she said at last in a plaintive tone, after she had spent a minute or so in vainly pursuing a large bright thing that looked sometimes like a doll and sometimes like a work-box, and was always in the shelf next above the one she was looking at.

Alice through the Looking Glass

I shall begin with a thesis that may be difficult to discuss without too much familiarity, the thesis that the history of sexuality is the history of its repression. Patriarchal voices can be summoned in evidence: Freud, in 1925:

The elimination of clitoridal sexuality is a necessary precondition for the development of feminity.

Acton, in 1857:

As a general rule a modest woman seldom desires any sexual gratification for herself. She submits to her husband but only to please him; and, but for the desire of maternity, would far rather be relieved from his attentions.[1]

The mode of confident generalization, of assertion, characterizes these statements. These are not the thoughts of trivial men, but the outcome of painstaking enquiry, of the close observation of the sick, the lunatic, the deviant. Theory can support them: the whole apparatus of the Oedipus complex and the castration complex which produce our painful and precarious entry into the world of gendered sexuality. These are thoughts wrested from the other side, from the world of an unrepressed or badly repressed sexuality which we must not know. Notice, too, how women seem to occupy some special place – 'femininity', 'the modest woman' – as though they had to be the particular targets of a repressive regime. But that doesn't make them the only targets. On the basis of careful observation, of clinical knowledge, Acton warns against the dangers of masturbation: it will lead to epilepsy or lunacy. This kind of thinking was the basis of those nice surgical interventions practiced by Dr. Flood of Massachusetts who in 1898 castrated twenty six boys suffering from 'epilepsy and masturbation' or 'masturbation with weakness of mind', or by Isaac Baker Brown, who set up the London Surgical Home in the 1860s to practice clitoridectomies on girls and women showing 'abnormal' signs of sexual desire.[2]

An understanding of history as the repression of sexuality enables us to get behind the facade of science, theory, and expertise that informs the statements of Freud and Acton. It enables us to see through the warnings of moralists and clerics about what is natural and unnatural. The same basic message is repeated throughout, 'sexuality must be repressed or society will die'.

At first this may seem a paradoxical injunction: how could an unrepressed sexuality, the force of procreation, lead to society's death? But what Freud saw precisely and Acton obscurely was that human sexuality was only contingently connected to the requirements of procreation. hence Acton's fears about masturbation as the wasting of a resource which should be properly, 'economically', invested in that procreation which would secure the inheritance of property. Hence, too, his fears about an active female sexuality, finding its pleasures in the clitoris, and quite baffling and defying the fragile ability of the penis to inseminate. Freud, of course, charted the route through which an 'infantile' sexuality, which could find its pleasures almost anywhere – in the arse or the mouth, in sucking or stuffing, touching or probing – was necessarily repressed in order to become a genital sexuality, combining, however precariously, pleasure with the requirements of procreation.[3] Hence, his assertion that the properly 'feminine' woman finds her pleasures in the vagina stimulated by the penis and not in the clitoris which, after all, as Freud well knew, didn't need a man to be happy. For Freud, unrepressed sexuality was a continent of pleasure which each of us could own but all must renounce because it was a force antithetical to social order. An unrepressed sexuality transformed the external environment with objects for gratification, to be curiously tested and then discarded or aggressively destroyed.

What has the history of sexuality as its repression to do with politics? To begin with, we could attend to a voice of indignation and complaint.

> With what sense does the parson claim the labour of the farmer?
> What are his nets, and guns, and traps. And how does he surround him
> With cold floods of abstraction, and with forests of solitude
> To build him castles and high spires. where kings and priests may dwell
> Till she who burns with youth, and knows no fixed lot, is bound
> In spells of law to one she loaths: and must she drag the chain
> Of life in weary lust! must chilling murderous thoughts obscure
> The clear heaven of her external spring? to bear the wintry rage
> Of a harsh terror driven to madness, bound to hold a rod
> Over her shrinking shoulders all the day; and all the night
> To turn the wheel of false desire ...

The voice is, of course, fictional, imaginary. It belongs to Oothoon, the mythical representative of female desire in William Blake's poem, *The Visions of the Daughters of Albion*, written in 1797.[4] Her speech is addressed to Bromion, representative of male lust and the rule to domination, and Theotormon, her lover, who has jealously rejected her as defiled after she has been raped by Bromion. The story represents in mythic form the fate of a woman who acts on desire, to be raped and then rejected. Oothoon has good reason to complain, but her complaint is also a diagnosis of why she has been hurt. What is offered is an account of repressive relations without recourse to the concept of repression as such. Oothoon's speech tells how the forms of sexual life reproduce and sustain other forms of life, social, economic, and intellectual. In a society where the parson claims 'the labour of the farmer', the man claims the sexual labour of the woman, justified by the 'spells of law' in a way which brands sexuality with alienation in what appears the most intimate area of life, ' ...and all the night/To turn the wheel of false desire'. Sexuality becomes a grotesque and sadistic drama, characterized by concealment and destructive pretence, in a society which requires untruth for its perpetuation. That this is repression, and not just hard luck, depends upon the imagining of a state of libidinal energy, the she 'who burns with youth, and knows no fixed lot', which is then trapped and perverted in the machinery of exploitation.

A political perception? Oothoon's speech makes the senses, the body, sexual energy a political subject, a subject of politics, because the body itself is engrossed in the struggle between freedom and constraint. The liberation of the body becomes a political objective, and the means of its realization nothing less than the entire transformation of society. The *imagination* of revolution is essential to this liberation of the body, and hence the utopian character of its politics, what Oothoon later envisions in the poem as a state of being 'Open to joy and delight wherever beauty appears'. But what can be held in imagination is altogether more difficult to translate into the terms of a specific political practice, if only because so many difficult questions arise: what is the 'body' in this imagination of it? Evidently not what falls sick and dies, but the site of an energy, a potential whose realization brings joy. Is there a politics specific to this 'body' or is its liberation the outcome of something like a marxist revolutionary practice which ideally brings about an equitable distribution of society's wealth and an end to the exploitation of labour?

What is at issue here is a form of idealism whose politics oppose the repression of sexuality to its liberation. I shall return to the structure and the problems of this idealism in discussing the work of Reich and Marcuse, but this needs to be done within the pressure of a different perspective, one which opposes sexual repression to a radical political practice.

Chapter 5 of *Civilization and Its Discontents* is the place, the moment of Freud's melancholy rejoinder to Communism. According to Freud, the Communist assumption that an equitable redistribution of property would bring about an end to aggression is based upon 'an untenable illusion' about the nature of human sexuality.[5] Freud's thesis about sexuality in *Civilisation and Its Discontents* is probably too well known to need detailed recapitulation here. Its character is complex, a matter of the combination of two classes of instincts, Eros and Thanatos. Eros, according to Laplache and Pontalis in their *Language of Psycho-analysis*, connotes

> the whole group of instincts which create or maintain organic unities, and this group must eventually include not only the sexual instincts in as much as they tend to preserve the species but also the self-preservative instincts which aim to maintain and assert the existence of the individual.

Thanatos is the death instinct and

> may lay claim ... to that aspect of human sexuality which Freud had recognised as definitive of human desire: its ineradicability, persistence, unrealistic nature and – from the economic point of view – its tendency to reduce tensions to zero.[6]

For Freud, then, sexuality, at the very least, is not a simple unity. It is characterized by doubleness and contradiction, by a pleasure in destruction as well as connection, by a craving for an end to stimuli as much as for their renewal and diversification. Moreover, the central thesis of *Civilization and Its Discontents* is that the basic instinctual organization informing human sexuality is in an unmodified form incompatible with social life. In order to effect a compromise between instinctual and sexual drives and the demands of social reality, sexuality is subject to various mechanisms, amongst which repression plays a primary role in so far as those forms of sexual desire and demand which are unacceptable in reality are repressed into the unconscious where they continue to have an active but fantastic life. Freud, in effect, tells us that we are all doomed to frustration.

Whatever outlets our repressed sexuality may find, whether it be in fantasy or the socially acceptable forms of heterosexuality, they are only substitutes for what we always wanted but could never have, those pleasures renounced in the repression of sexuality.

Repression and its consequences are ubiquitous. No change in the distribution of property and the character of social relations can affect it. What can be affected is the modes in which, for example, the aggressive component in sexuality finds acceptable, sublimated expressions. In this respect sexuality becomes the ironic antithesis to communist aspirations because even if a society characterized by an equitable distribution of wealth, by sexual freedom and universal peace were realized, it would, according to Freud, bring about an end to those forms of natural rivalry and individual competition which are amongst the acceptable forms of outlet for aggressive sexual desires. But not an end to that particular form of the drive; instead it would be turned inward producing self-torture, guilt and misery amongst individuals in a society whose material conditions and political order testified everywhere to the possibility of happiness.

Freud's encounter with communism can be read in terms of a variety of cultural configurations: as the clash between utopia and melancholy, between the hopeful and the fed-up, between those who think there's still more to be done and those who think too much has been done already. But it's also the emblematic work of a divergence and resistance between a logic of psychoanalysis and a marxist logic of practice. Psychoanalytic sexuality remains inaccessible to practice, in so far as that is conceived in its classic marxist form, as the dialectic between knowing the world and changing it. In so far as the conception is, or should be, at the core of a marxist politics, psychoanalytic sexuality is outside politics. It is not amenable to a political will, although it can take that will and make it into a vehicle of its own sublimated expression. This formulation of the divergence between psychoanalysis and marxism is no doubt crude and without mediation, but it seems to me that even when the mediations have been built into the account, we don't have a sexual politics but a split between politics and sexuality, in which the conception of practice itself, in so far as it's applied to sexuality, shifts away from politics towards the formalities and intimacies of 'talking cure'.

Of course there have been numerous attempts to incorporate marxism and psychoanalysis within one conceptual model, despite the evident differences in the way the two discourses distribute the senses of subject and agency, change and purpose.[7] A primary motive in this work has been to restore sexuality to a political history (a history capable of engendering a politics). To think, though, of a primary motive here may be to risk simplification, and the notion of a conceptual model runs a similar risk. Rather we find a body of work in which the terms of marxism and psychoanalysis are set up in a relation of exchange and modification, in which whatever is proposed by way of answer then begs further questions. The writings of Reich and Marcuse can be taken to illustrate this process in more detail.

A history of failure accompanies the works of Reich and Marcuse as its more or less explicit counterpoint and occasion. The failure consists in a series of defeats for European socialism: the First World war, the suppression of the German revolutionary movement, the use of fascism, the Cold War and the long arc of capitalist prosperity after 1945. Nor were these defeats in any simple sense the outcome of a brutal repression of socialist parties, although that had its part to play. Both Reich and Marcuse, in different contexts, were confronted with the problem of the persistence of authoritarianism in political states that enjoyed a measure of democratic rights. Why did fascism enjoy active support or, at the least, passive acceptance amongst social groups whose interests, according to a marxist calculus, were opposed to such a regime? Why, in the post-war United States, did a country enjoying an unprecedented material abundance, and again, according to marxist prediction, ripe for the transition to socialism, show not the least sign of making such a change? Given the availability of marxist analysis, what was it that made the proletariat of advanced industrial nations continue to acquiesce in their own exploitation?

Old, intractable questions – and, according to Reich and Marcuse, their answer was not to be found in a Leninist analysis of a failure in the tactics and strategy of revolutionary parties, but in the secret of the unconscious and repressed sexuality. Hence, another configuration of the relations of history, politics and sexuality according to repression, one which entailed the mapping of a psychoanalytic conception of history on to a marxist conception. For Marcuse, sexual repression was an archaic necessity, a precondition for the overcoming of scarcity. Marcuse's account of historical development establishes the terms of a dialectic central to his work: material advance is purchased at the cost of psychic mutilation. The mastery of human and non-human nature diminishes our capacity for sensuous enjoyment. Analagous themes run through Reich's equally speculative history: the socially necessary process of accumulation becomes bound to a regressive sexuality. Accumulation becomes a desire antagonistic to the general social good, a desire that 'avails itself of the anal tendencies which were brought out by sexual restriction'.[8]

For both writers the history of twentieth century capitalism is marked by a critical intensification of the dialectic of progress and regression which is an informing principle of their critique. What were once necessities have now become dangerous liabilities: Reich's 'Masochistic Character', the product of an epochal experience of domination and repression, strongly disposed to identify with the strong leader, compensating for a sense of inferiority and weakness in a sadistic rage against vulnerable social groups; or Marcuse's account of a society traversed by surplus repression, the mechanism whereby one class dominates another in the absence of any rational requirement either for the maintenance of social life or the development of material wealth. Surplus repression takes the body's capacity for sexual pleasure as its particular target, and the consequent thwarting of the sexual drive produces a vengeful aggression which, reacting against a joyless life, can lay waste the bases of social existence.

What emerges from the work of Reich and Marcuse is an account of capitalism in its apocalyptic phase. The contest between socialism and capitalism is transformed into the struggle between life and death, its messianic solution, the liberation of sexuality,

> the abolition of poverty and toil ... in a universe where the sensuous, the playful, the calm and the beautiful become the forms of existence, and thereby the Form of the society itself.[9]

Rehearsing this critique now seems like bringing an ageing actor on stage for his final bow.

The critique had its moment of ideological force in the student movement of the late 1960s. A revolutionary theory seemed to coincide with a revolutionary practice. It produced a politics of demonstration, a staging of unrepressed energy in the face of a repressive society. For a while, too, bourgeois society played its part as protagonist in the drama, combining moral outrage with tear gas and the truncheon.

Then an unforeseen character appeared, the capitalist entrepreneur who spoke the language of sexual liberation in the columns of *Playboy* and *Hustler*, in the production of blue movies and sex manuals. This produced a serious problem for the critique in that it seemed to question a central assumption, that the capitalist order was necessarily an order of sexual repression. Of course it could be argued that this advertisement of sexuality was not a genuine sexual liberation, merely one of those periodic phases of hedonistic licence produced by a capitalism confident of its prosperity, but then, in practice, it became difficult to tell what the authentic freedom of Eros would be like – unless the whole critique could be re-read as a myth, where an unrepressed sexuality did not connote any particular form of sexual behaviour, but rather symbolized an energy or mode of being which resisted a process noted by Marx long ago, the tendency of capitalism to convert the relation between human beings into a relation between commodities.[10] But even the myth found its disillusioning answer as the conversion of sexuality into a commodity proceeded apace, despite protests from various unrevolutionary quarters. Sexuality was for sale like it had never been before, and never before had it been so greedily consumed. In this confusion, fragments of Marcuse and Reich, although certainly not the whole critique, could be converted into sales-talk.

There were other, serious, problems with the argument that sexual liberation and the overthrow of capitalism were linked processes. One has to do with a historical thesis, central to both Reich and Marcuse, that sexual repression is linked to the struggle to overcome material scarcity. This produces a corresponding prognosis for an authentic socialism, a society characterized by material abundance in which poverty and toil are abolished and an unrepressed sexuality can flourish. There is at once a conceptual problem here in an account which reads scarcity and abundance as absolute and not relative terms. Further, as a prediction of economic tendency, the account seems hopelessly naive in a world where the majority face starvation and capitalist economies remain bound in the cycle of over-production and recession. Under these circumstances, to propose that socialism awaits material abundance is, in effect, to postpone socialism forever.[11]

As an account of sexuality, the critique encounters further difficulties. Both Reich and Marcuse give an honourable and even heroic role to women in their writings. In the *Mass Psychology of Fascism* Reich claimed that 'sexually-awakened women, affirmed and recognized as such, would mean the complete collapse of authoritarian ideology'.[12] Towards the end of his life, Marcuse found in the women's liberation movement a renewed possibility of revolutionary agency. Where the working-class, the young, the student movement had failed, perhaps women would succeed. But to propose a heroic role for women in this way bears a tenuous relation to the political exigencies of feminist struggle, if only because women occupy a symbolic place in Reich and Marcuse's writing centred in the opposition between masculine qualities of brutality and domiantion and feminine qualities of 'non-violence, receptivity and tenderness'.[13] Yet, as we shall see in more detail later, it is precisely the oppression of being a symbol in a masculine imagination that has become a subject of feminist critique.

The history of sexuality is the history of its repression: as the basis for a radical critique and practice this thesis now seems peculiarly vulnerable, overtaken by events and processes whose complexity cannot be accounted for by its particular logic. The result is speculative history: an account of sexuality which moves uneasily between analytic and symbolic modes; a politics that is utopian and theatrical. Whether the problems that result can be overcome remains to be seen, but, for the moment, I want to return to a major conceptual problem, that the idea of repression itself misconceives the relations between sexual life and social regulation. Foucault's work revolves around this critical perception and provides an alternative thesis connecting sexuality to history: the history of sexuality is the history of a discourse.

The attempt to counter the argument that sexuality is to be understood, historically, in terms of its repression gives shape to Foucault's first, introductory volume of *The History of Sexuality*. A preliminary strategy is to point up a seeming paradox in the repression thesis: why in a society ostensibly characterized by sexual repression is sexuality so audibly discussed? Why is it replayed in the different cultural media? Why are psychoanalysts paid to listen to people 'impart the secrets of their sex'?[14] Not, according to Foucault, because sex has been repressed – rather the fact that it is described as 'repressed', a 'secret' is a further stimulus to the production of discourse about it. It is one amongst the many ways in which we have learnt to be garrulous about sex. This, in him, raises a doubt about the critical force of the concept of repression: does it stand outside the dominant mode of organizing sexuality in modern capitalist societies or is it not, rather, another local manoeuvre in that organization?

Foucault's answer to this question develops along three related lines of enquiry. The first is historical, a matter of setting the record straight, of indicating the body of evidence which would call into question the validity of repression as an historical explanation of the fate of sexuality. The second is theoretical, concerned with the relation between knowledge and its objects, and, in this particular case, with the kind of reality that can be attributed to the concept of sexuality. The third combines history, theory, and politics in its concern with the nature of power, and the validity of repression as a concept which can explain the relation betwen sexuality and power in modern societies.

Modern sexuality, according to Foucault, has a number of historical origins, some which may at first sight seem unlikely. The reformation of the confession and the sacrament of penance after the Council of Trent is one such starting point. In the reformed confession the probing of the relation between sex and sin becomes less a matter of the description of an act and more an investigation of a motive, of the first stirring of sexual desire in an image or a daydream, or a moment of unexpected pleasure. There is a corresponding alteration in the language of confession, away from an explicit naming of an act toward a more euphemistic, indirect speech about a motive, but this is not to be understood in any simple sense as an effect of repression. Rather it marks an extension of power into the form of subjectivity itself and one that has momentous consequences:

> It was here, perhaps, that the injunction, so peculiar to the West, was laid down for the first time in the form of a general constraint. I am not talking about the obligation to admit to violations of the laws of sex, as required by traditional penance; but of the nearly infinite task of telling – telling oneself and another, as often as possible, everything that might concern the interplay of innumerable pleasures, sensations, and thoughts which through the body and the soul, had some affinity with sex ... An imperative was established: Not only will you confess to acts contravening the law, but you will seek to transform your desire, your every desire, into discourse.[15]

This establishes one important form of modern sexuality: the requirement that the person become transparent to power by confessing everything he knows; the self becomes a sacrificial offering to an insatiable authority. But if this marks the extension of power into what may seem most intimate and private, Foucault notes that its detachment from Christian spirituality was caused by a 'public interest', the emergence toward the beginning of the eighteenth century of 'a political, economic, and technical incitement to talk about sex'. 'Sex' became a subject of administration, in the regulation of population, for example, in the concern of educational reforms with children's sexuality, or in the concern of doctors with the treatment of nervous disorders whose energies are perceived as sexual, the products of 'excess'.

The manifold effects of these historical developments are not a repression of sexuality but its opposite: social life becomes saturated with sex. There is no encounter, no act, no institution which is not traversed by sexuality. In particular, Foucault notes four great 'strategic unities', points of exchange between power, knowledge, and sexuality: the 'hysterization of women's bodies', their identification with sexuality; the 'pedagogization of children's sex', a sex at once natural and dangerous, to be carefully monitored in the child's development; the 'socialization of procreative behaviour', the fact that fertility becomes a matter of public policy; the 'psychiatrization of perverse pleasure', the pursuit of illic normal and pathological forms of the sexual instinct. Each of these forms corresponds to a different sexual character: 'the hysterical woman, the masturbating child, the Malthusian couple and the perverse adult'.[17] Each of these characters, in turn, marks a point where power and knowledge make use of people's sex, and, in a process of historical convergence, each turns up in the family which then becomes, according to Foucalt, a 'hotbed of sexuality' and not the place of its repression.

There are numerous other points which could be noted in Foucault's historical account: for example, the antagonistic and complicit relation between the 'deployment of alliance' conceived with rules of kinship, the inheritance of property and names, the maintenance of law and the 'deployment of sexuality', restless, innovative, hedonistic, an economic force not through the inheritance and circulation of wealth but in its concern with 'the body that produces and consumes'.[18] But, for the moment, I want to look at some of the theoretical implications of Foucault's history, and, in particular, what it tells about the nature of sexuality itself.

Foucault does not perceive sexuality as a primordial force which threatens social order unless it is repressed:

Sexuality must not be thought of as a kind of natural given which power holds in check ... It is the name that can be given to a historical construct: not a furtive reality that is difficult to grasp but a great surface network in which the stimulation of bodies, the intensification of pleasures, the incitement to discourse, the formation of special knowledges, the strengthening of controls and resistances, are linked to one another ...[19]

Nor is there something called 'sex' which exists prior to sexuality such that the latter constitutes a knowledge of the former. The relationship is rather the reverse: 'sex' is the culminating achievement of the historical construct of sexuality, one of its most powerful strategies, an imaginary unity, something that is everywhere and nowhere, which we have to know in order to know ourselves. 'Sex' is at once an impossible obligation and a ubiquitous craving, a ruse of power in that:

> ... it made it possible to invest the representation of the relationships of power to sexuality, causing the latter to appear not in its essential and positive relation to power, but as being rooted in a specific and irreducible urgency which power tries as best it can to dominate; thus the idea of 'sex' makes it possible to evade what gives 'power' its power. It enables one to conceive power solely as law and taboo.[20]

This passage repeats a key term in Foucault's writing, 'power', without necessarily making it clear what the term might mean. Elsewhere in *The History of Sexuality* Foucault writes more explicitly about power, although the term remains for me at least shadowed by a certain metaphysical presumption. Power seems to be for Foucault an irreducible social datum. Its origin is not to be found in the economic organization of life, either in the 'first' or the 'last' instance. This is not the only sign of the distance of Foucault's account of power from a marxist conception. Thus power, at the outset, does not mean the exploitation of one class by another, nor is it what an Althusserian would understand by ideological or repressive state apparatuses, the 'institutions and mechanisms that ensure the subservience of the citizens of a given state'.

Power is ubiquitous, immanent in all social relations. It is part of the difficulty of definition here that Foucault has recourse to so many statements of what power is not:

> ... Power is everywhere; not because it embraces everything, but because it comes from everywhere ... One needs to be nominalistic, no doubt: power is not an institution, and not a structure; neither is it a certain strength we are endowed with; it is the name that one attributes to a complex strategical situation in a particular society.[21]

And if that leaves you gasping from abstractions, it's worth remembering that sexuality is just such a

> complex strategical situation ... an especially dense transfer point for relations of power: between men and women, young people and old people, parents and offspring, teachers and students, priests and laity, an administration and a population.[22]

But if power is to be understood at a local level in the first instance, not a matter of simple coercion but as a point of 'transfer', a highly unstable contest, a matter of constant negotiation and re-negotiation 'in the interplay of non-egalitarian and mobile relations', it nonetheless crystallises into historically determinate forms. Here we can begin to measure something of the instability of Foucault's distance from marxism, because *The History of Sexuality*, like other of his works, can be read as a particularly detailed and forceful account of the rise and consolidation of bourgeois hegemony. The place of sexuality in this history can be best understood in terms of one of Foucault's innovative additions to an understanding of social class, that 'one of the primordial forms of class consciousness is the affirmation of the body'.[23] Sexuality is then the historical construct through which the bourgeosie affirmed its own body, always in relation, it has to be added, to other 'alien' class bodies: the aristocracy as a body in need of regeneration, the proletarian body as initially a matter of indifference,and subsequently as something in need of careful regulation and shaping. The work of creating different class bodies was conducted through administrative

efforts, the application of medical and scientific knowledge
about hygiene and correct family size, in implicit forms of
marriage, all supplemented by imaginary creations which,
across a range of writings, both 'realistic' and 'fantastic',
established particular images of alien class bodies: the
aristocratic as at once emaciated, sterile and predatory; the
proletarian as both robust and underfed, healthily productive
or in danger of degeneration through 'excess' and
'animality'.[24] Psychoanalysis and the discovery of repression
mark an important moment in this history of discriminating
class bodies. Foucault describes this moment in a series of
pointed oppositions, all having to do with the different ways
that incest was permitted and prohibited in the late nineteenth
century:

> At the moment when Freud was uncovering the nature of Dora's
> desire and allowing it to be put into words, preparations were
> being made to undo those reprehensible proximities in other
> social sectors: on the one hand the father was elevated into an
> object of compulsory love, but on the other hand, if he was a loved
> one, he was … a fallen one in the eyes of the law … Those who had
> lost the exclusive privilege of worrying over their sexuality
> henceforth had the privilege [through the instruments of
> psychoanalysis] of experiencing more than others the thing that
> had prohibited it and of possessing the method which made it
> possible to remove the repression.[25]

Or, psychoanalysis permits the bourgeoisie to reach the parts
that other classes can't reach.

But, according to Foucault, the history of sexuality cannot be
understood in terms of class hegemony alone. The latter is an
episode in the description of a larger historical trajectory, one
whose conceptualization draws upon the effort of various
histories and sociologies to distinguish between old and
modern forms of society. Where others have seen this
opposition in terms of a contrast between agrarian and industrial, or feudal and bourgeois societies, Foucault subsumes
these distinctions into an opposition between different modes
of power: on the one hand 'the ancient right to take life or let
live', or the modern power 'to foster life or disallow it to the

point of death'.[26] This 'ancient right' finds its embodiment in the institutional forms of sovereignty and the law, whose power consists in

> a right to appropriate a portion of the wealth, a tax of products, goods and services, labour and blood, levied on the subjects. Power in this instance was essentially a right of seizure.[27]

Modern power, by contrast, does not take what is already there, or exercise a prohibition; it is productive, investing the forms of life through the implementation of various technologies,

> a power bent on generating forces, making them grow, and ordering them, rather than one dedicated to impeding them, making them submit, or destroying them.[28]

The relation between these two modes of power is too complex to detail here. The one, of course, has not simply replaced the other. The old forms of sovereignty and the law can be antagonistic to the new technologies of power, or they can collude with them in deceptive ways, and nowhere more so than in the area of sexuality which, according to Foucault, a radical critique fixated on the idea of repression falls prey to a limited conception of the power it is ostensibly addressing. Indeed, Foucault finds a similar limitation in an apparently opposite view, associated with Lacanian psychoanalysis, which instead of defining desire as energy which is repressed, sees it rather as something which is constituted by prohibition, the effect of a law which makes desire something that can never be fulfilled. Both views are limited because they work with a conception of power as interdiction, with the model based on law and sovereignty. Nor is this one-sided conception of power the result of a simple error. It is the result of an ideology which masks the operations of technological power:

> ... power is tolerable only on condition that it mask a substantial part of itself. Its success is proportional to its ability to hide its own mechanisms ... For its secrecy is not in the nature of an abuse; it is indispensable to its operation. Not only because power

imposes secrecy on those whom it dominates, but because it is perhaps just as indispensable to the latter: would they accept it if they did not see it as a mere limit placed on their desire, leaving a measure of freedom – however slight – intact? Power as pure limit set on freedom is, at least in our society, the general form of its acceptability.[29]

Foucault's work, then, provides the historical and theoretical basis for a statement of these reservations and doubts silenced by the omnipresent cult of sexuality and the various projects of self-knowledge and liberation which have grouped around it. But is that the sum total of its political effect? What, if any, are the political recommendations that might be derived from *The History of Sexuality*? Foucault's work provides no obvious answer to this question. This may be a matter of tactical reserve on Foucault's part, a refusal to identify his work with a radical culture which has been so strong in utopian projects and political 'lines', so weak in actual political achievement. Not just that, however, because Foucault's conception of power as something that 'comes from everywhere', something mobile and ubiquitous, to be grasped, both conceptually and politically, at its local level of operation, makes it difficult, if not impossible, to occupy a theoretical position which could either predict or dictate a correct political practice. According to Foucault, resistance is both intrusive to the operations of power and not predictable in advance. Thus, the legal, psychiatric and literary discourses of the nineteenth century concerned with the classification of sexual 'perversions' contributed to their social control. But they also enabled

the formation of a 'reverse discourse': homosexuality began to speak on its own behalf, to demand that its legitimacy or 'naturality' be acknowledged, often in the same, using the same categories by which it was disqualified ...[30]

and this is not because discourse and the power it bears develop according to a dialectic law of contradiction, but because of a particular conjuncture in which the knowledge of perversity was now directed by one particular interest, now by another and opposing interest.

Foucault's work displaces the connection between historical enquiry, utopian imaginings, and political recommendation which characterized the radical critique of sexual repression. Indeed some of his most trenchant criticisms centre on the delusions of 'liberation'; that, for example, by confessing our sex we free it from the constraints of power:

> ... one has to have an inverted image of power in order to believe that all those voices which have spoken so long in our civilisation – repeating the formidable injunction to tell what one is and what one does, what one recollects and what one has forgotten, what one is thinking and what one thinks he is thinking – are speaking to us of freedom.[31]

This is not the only cherished assumption to be called into question. Central terms of marxist theory and political practice, 'revolution', 'class struggle', both of which connected the liberation of sexuality with wider political and social goals, are themselves demoted by Foucault. Revolution and class struggle are possible outcomes of a particular configuration of power in society, but they are not the terms to which an understanding of power can be reduced. Yet this scepticism towards a radical attitude which connects sexual liberation to the freedom achieved through revolutionary class struggle has its paradoxical effect: scepticism about a revolutionary theory of history, politics and sexuality does not lead to the suppression of a revolutionary aspiration in Foucault's writing. This emerges in one of the few cryptic political recommendations in *The History of Sexuality*:

> We must not think by saying yes to sex, one says no to power; on the contrary, one tracks along the course laid out by the general deployment of sexuality. It is the agency of sex that we must break away from, if we aim – through a tactical reversal of the various mechanisms of sexuality – to counter the grip of power with the claims of bodies, pleasures, and knowledges, in their multiplicity and their possibility of resistance. The rallying point for the counter attack against the deployment of sexuality ought not to be sex-desire, but bodies and pleasures.[32]

This passage seems to reverse Foucault's earlier arguments. Where we had been warned against conceiving power as a 'binary and all-encompassing opposition between rulers and ruled', we find here a binary opposition between the solidarity of a 'we' or 'us' seeking to countermand the anonymous 'grip of power'. The mood of exhortation and admonition, coming appropriately enough at the conclusion of the work, renews the relation between the subject of sex and the form of the sermon which Foucault had earlier noted as a pervasive way in which the 'agency of sex' entered into discourse.[33] Foucault writes from a discursive position which he had earlier criticized, and, not least, in holding out 'the promise of a certain felicity' in the freeing of 'bodies and pleasures' from the tyranny of 'sex-desire'. This, in its turn, seems approximate to the utopian prospect held out by the reduced critique of repression. What Marcuse had described as the transformation of the body from an instrument of labour into an instrument of pleasure comes close to Foucault's advocacy of 'bodies and pleasures'. This may evidence a return of the repressed thesis or repression in Foucault's own thinking, as though there is something stubborn within it which survives Foucault's many telling criticisms and then speaks in their despite: something about a pleasure in the body which does stand on the other side of power and symbolizes a point of release from the anxieties about manipulation and exploitation which come with the knowledge of power.

Foucault produces a history of sexuality as the history of interconnected discourses by way of what we can now see as an ambivalent critique of the thesis that the history of sexuality is the history of its repression. This latter can be read as the sub-text which is transformed by Foucault's own writing. What is remarkable in a work published in 1976 is the absence of any specific address to feminist writing on the history and politics of sexuality. This may again be evidence of a tactical reticence on Foucault's part, an unwillingness to be identified as either 'pro' or 'anti' feminist. It may be that in a later volume of *The History of Sexuality* Foucault will take up the history of feminism but, whatever the reasons for this silence, there are, nevertheless, ideas in *The History of Sexuality* which have a bearing on developments in feminist thought and politics. His work therefore can serve as a point of transition to what will be a necessarily brief set of comments on a body of thought which is vital to any account of the relations between history, politics, and sexuality.

> ... what we have seen has been a very real process of struggle; life as a political object was in a sense taken at face value and turned back against the system that was bent on controlling it. It was life more than law that became the issue of political struggles, even if the latter were formulated through affirmations concerning rights.[34]

The characteristic of modern power, according to Foucault, is to turn life into a 'political object'. Once this is so, women become decisive political subjects, wherever the power to regulate and invest life develop. This is not a matter of choice, nor is it obviously to be equated with some sudden accession to power by women in the recent historical past. The 'power to foster life or disallow it' transforms natural inevitabilities, whose effects might be mitigated but never controlled, into political domains where power can be transferred or contested.

The emergence of a politics of reproduction is an obvious example. Malthus's theory of the inverse relation between the growth of population and the growth of food supply is an early instance and the development can be traced through the reductive identification of women with their reproductive capacity in nineteenth century medicine, into the eugenics movement, and then to the recent struggles by women to be the arbiters of their own fertility.

The story is by no means one of simple radical advance: a new power is discovered in the various medical technologies which can control fertility; the modern state assumes a responsibility for ensuring the 'healthy' reproduction of the race and this in turn produces a whole network of institutions and discourses which can exhort women to bear children or tell them not to, which establishes definitions of the right and wrong times to have children and the special responsibilities which accrue to women once they're born. But within the circuits of power thus established some women contest their definition by medical and administrative power, and demand control of the knowledge and technologies which concern their fertility: 'a woman's right to choose'. Or women campaign around a different slogan, the 'right to life', demanding against modern power that the development of the foetus be returned to the cycle of natural inevitability. Modern power, as described by Foucault, establishes a new relation between radical and reactionary politics. It does not in any sense produce a politics exclusive to women, but it does define women's relation to power in a way which the older politics of sovereignty and the law does not. In the latter women are tokens of exchange, there to confirm that a particular negotiation of power had been completed, and thus define their public role. In the former, the 'power to foster life and disallow it', a struggle develops around the control of fertility in which women can become political contestants against an ambiguous opponent, sometimes the state, sometimes definitions of nature, sometimes a strange amalgam of both. This struggle has recently taken an apocalyptic form in the nuclear arena, which as Foucault reminds us:

> is now at the end point of this process: the power to expose a whole population to death is the underside of the power to guarantee an individual's existence ... But the existence in question is no longer the juridical existence of sovereignty; at stake is the biological existence of a population.[35]

It is not surprising then that women, at Greenham Common and elsewhere, should have a special place in the struggle against nuclear weapons, and not only as symbols of what is vulnerable to power, but as the politically responsible guardians of life engaged in a struggle against the dream of genocide that is sustained by nuclear weapons.

What does this indicate about the history of sexuality? At first, something obvious and easily overlooked: the history of sexuality is about the reproduction of the species. One important contribution of the women's movement has been to remind us of this and Foucault takes up the reminder. Its significance is disclosed in at least two ways: it supplies an absence in the history which draws on the concept of repression, where biological reproduction is subordinated to the question of sexual pleasure and its denial. Secondly, it marks a decisive transformation in the history of sexuality itself, one that has already been noted in the complex process which made biological reproduction into a political issue.

In modern societies, this produces a double relation between biological and cultural sexuality. On the one hand, human culture is deemed to transform biological sex, whether by mechanisms of repression or discourse. The 'problematic' of this approach centres on questions of gender identity, pleasure, and desire. On the other hand, the nuclear situation and developments in genetics propose a different relation: human culture is charged with the preservation as well as the transformation of biological existence. How this very recent development is affecting human sexual definition is very hard to tell; that it is seems to me beyond dispute.

One of the strengths of feminism has been in its capacity to work in terms of both these relations between cultural and biological existence. If, now, some women define their sex in terms of a strategic responsibility for the preservation of life, it is equally true that the transformation of biological sexual difference into culturally gendered identity is a major theme of feminist thought, and has its corollary in a third major thesis about the history of sexuality, not as a history of repression, nor of discourse, but the systematic exploitation of women by men.

This is not the place for a detailed résumé of the evidence that has been put forward to prove the oppression of women and the manifold ways they have sought to resist it.[36] But, in noting the varying relations between histories and politics of sexuality, an important difference emerges from this third form of the history of sexuality. It has been connected to a diversity of political practice, one that includes those utopian and theatrical forms connected to the account of sexuality as repressed, but goes on to more immediate confrontations with power, whether it be the power men assume in sexual relations, the power the state assumes over the administration of contraception and abortion, or the various powers that exclude women from cultural, political and professional life.

This comprehensive political engagement draws strength from the historical knowledge of women's struggles and from a theory which identifies a whole system of power called patriarchy, one whose relation with other marxist and liberal theories of power is continually debated. Without wishing for a moment then to deny the complex theoretical issues disclosed by the women's movement, it is the case that problems of theory have not stifled the creation of an actual, rather than a speculative or imaginary politics. One reason why this is so may have to do with a delicate and difficult distinction between two related terms, repression and oppression.[37] In actual use the two terms can become synonymous, but they do, nonetheless, designate different modalities in the operation of power.

If, for a moment, we return to *Civilization and Its Discontents*, we can see that for Freud repression is synonymous with being human. Put another way, it is the exercise of a power of prohibition which gives birth to the self, however traumatic that birth might be. If Reich and Marcuse try to give a more historic title to repression, and more particularly to trace its mode of operation within a phase of capitalist society, it still works to produce what, for example, Reich called the 'masochistic character'. Both thinkers are then confronted with the particular dilemma of how to disentangle a self from the powers that constitute it. The intractable nature of this dilemma may well account for the utopian drift of their thought and the increasingly forlorn pursuit of some form of operational agency outside the seemingly all-encompassing power of capitalism, whether it be in youth, the student movement, art or the orgone box. The problem, of course, is not one of thought alone but of the particular history in which it unfolds, that long crisis of political practice which Perry Anderson has analysed as a constitutive theme and limitation of western Marxism.[38] Recourse to an analysis based upon the links between sexuality and repression has, more often than not, intensified this problem rather than solved it.

If not exactly by contrast, then certainly as a matter of

marked difference, an influential strand in feminist analysis has emphasised women's oppression in a way that gives the term conceptual parity, if not priority, to repression. Oppression figures a relation between power and the self, whereby the former does not constitute the latter so much as frustrate it. Nor is this a frustration of sexuality in the sense that it creates that desire-which-can-never-be-fulfilled. It is the frustration of potentials that can be named and known, and whose overcoming can be practically conceived as a matter of access to this kind of work or that kind of power which has hitherto been held as an exclusive privilege by men. Oppression leaves a measure of selfhood free from but denied by power. It may be that the concept of oppression in feminist analysis reflects the existing political militancy which has surrounded its use. But it has also enabled that militancy by creating a discourse which has held open a place for political agency emanating from a self defined as not entirely formed by power, and, as such, it holds out a route from thought to action where consequences have been optimistically stated by Brecht in his poem, *The Gordian Knot*,

> ... an answer less often suffices to end the world of a question than a deed.[39]

Except, of course, that affirmation is not come by so easily, least of all at a point where politics and sexuality converge. The difficulties of holding to any analysis which will do justice to the differential relations of history, politics, and sexuality can succumb to a fantasy which projects feminism or the woman's movement as a unified theoretical and political force, the solution to all our problems. Some of Lacan's later writings, *A Love Letter* and *The Seminar* of 21 January 1975, describe and dissect the masculine character of that fantasy:

> ... the more man may ascribe to the woman in confusion with God, that is, in confusion with what it is she comes from, the less he hates, the lesser he is, and since after all, there is no love without hate, the less he loves.[40]

a sentence, sufficiently dialectical, cryptic and pessimistic to point up the difficulties for men in establishing a political relation to feminism which is not overridden by fantasy relations.

Lacan's work can also serve as a reminder of the current divergences within feminist theories of 'the subject'. Amongst the theories which attempt to explain how biological sexual division becomes cultural gender difference, I want to mention two accounts whose disagreements about the nature of the subject seem to replay, although in different terms, the argument between Freud and communism. On the one hand, Althusser's theory of ideology as 'the representation' of the Imaginary relationship of individuals to their Real conditions of existence' is one starting point for an analysis which is concerned with the way current modes of representation define women as subjects subordinate to men whether as housewives, sex-objects, etc.[41] The power to define identity is attributed to a structure of images or image-like representations and produces a political practice which seeks to change how women are identified, and how they identify themselves by changing the modes of their representation. The Lacanian account, by contrast, stresses a different relation between the subject and representation in so far as the subject is always represented in language through a process of division and splitting.

> The subject is figured in symbolism by a stand-on or substitute, whether we have to do with the personal pronoun 'I', with the name that is given him, or with the denomination 'son of ' (sic) ... The subject mediated by language is unremedially divided because it has been excluded from the symbolic chain at the very moment at which it becomes represented in it.[42]

Freud's account of the genesis of sexual identity in repression and substitute gratifications is deliberately transposed here into an analysis of the relations between the subject and his or her representation in language such that the substitutive character of symbolism occasions the production of an unconscious which is composed, so to speak, of all that part of the subject which is left unrepresented. The acquisiton of language is simultaneously a point of repression and alienation, not the expression of a subject but its division, and one which has a particular bearing on sexuality in so far as it is within language, according to Lacan, that gender division is inscribed, but not in a relation of parity between the masculine and the feminine in so far as the latter stands to the former in a relation of positive to negative. Feminine 'identity' becomes a paradox: 'woman is what man is not'. Although Lacan's purpose is certainly not to recommend this process so much as to expose its operations in sustaining an hallucinated sexuality, the question of how things might be different becomes difficult indeed. Women's representation in language can no longer be conceived in terms of a change in what is represented; showing woman as they really are, or might be beyond the fantasies of men. The task enjoined is nothing less than a revolution in forms of language itself, one which replaces a relation between the subject premissed on division and less with

> a refusal of division which gives the woman access to a different strata of language, where words and things are not differentiated, and the real of the material body threatens or holds off women's access to prohibition and the law.[43]

It's as well, perhaps, to end with the possibility of such a revolution while noting, too, that the relation between Lacan and the French feminists, Montrelay and Ingary, seem to repeat the conversion of melancholy into utopian which connects Freud's work to that of Reich and Marcuse. Otherwise I'm left with continuing difficulties, not conclusion. It should be evident that the terms history, sexuality, and politics are engaged in an intricate dance which has at least two repeated motifs. Firstly, sexuality as a concept seems to offer reverse accounts of the relations between power and pleasure: on the one hand, no pleasure without power (Foucault); on the other, sexuality as the dream of pleasures beyond the grip of power (Marcuse, Reich). Secondly, there is the continuing difficulty of finding the terms which will mediate between the sexual subject, repressed, divided, de-centred, and the subject of a radical politics, one capable of knowing the world and changing it. In the absence of mediation, sexuality, which is nothing if not the science of substitution, itself produces a surrogate for political practice. This indeed may be its function in a radical culture whose ostensible commitment to social liberation comes into conflict with the privilege which permits the articulation of a global purpose in the first place. The consequent political paralysis can be compensated for by replaying the archaic goals of marxism – an end to economic exploitation, the overthrow of the bourgeoisie as a ruling class – in a semi-private and narcissistic world of the body and its desires. Liberating sex then becomes the bad faith of a radicalism incapable of achieving its social and political tasks.

References

1 Sigmund Freud, 'Some Psychological Consequences of the Anatomical Distinction between the Sexes', *Complete Psychological Works of Freud*, edited by J. Strachey, London, 1961, Volume 19, pp. 252, 255.
W. Acton, *The Functions and Disorders of the Reproductive Organs*, Sixth edition, 1875, pp. 212-13, quoted in B. Easlea, *Science and Sexual Oppression*, London, 1981, p. 130.
2 See B. Easlea, op. cit., pp. 130-136.
3 See S. Freud, *Three Essays on the Theory of Sexuality*, London, 1953.
4 W. Blake, *The Visions of the Daughters of Albion*, Plate 5, 11. 17-32, *The Poetry and Prose of William Blake*, edited by D.V. Erdman, New York, 1970. Thanks to my colleague David Aers for drawing my attention to this passage.
5 S. Freud, *Civilization and its Discontents*, translated by J. Strachey, 1963.
6 J. Laplache and J.B. Pontalis, *The Language of Psycho-Analysis*, translated by D. Nicholson-Smith, London, 1980, p.20.
7 Apart from the Works of Reich and Marcuse which are discussed in what follows, see also A. Foreman, *Femininity as Alienation*, London, 1970, and E. Zaretsky, *Capitalism, the Family and Personal Life*, London, 1976, and for an eloquent attempt to relate Lacan's work to marxism, see F. Jameson, 'Imaginary and Symbolic in Lacan', *Yale French Studies*, Number 55/56, 1977, pp. 338-395.
8 W. Reich, 'The Imposition of Sexual Morality', *Sex-Pol Essays*, edited by L. Baxandall, New York, 1972, p. 230. For Marcuse see *Eros and Civilization*, London, 1969, and *One Dimensional Man*, London, 1964.
9 H. Marcuse, *An Essay on Liberation*, London, 1969, p. 25.
10 K. Marx, *Capital*, volume 1, London, 1974, p. 77.
11 For the relativity of scarcity and abundance see J.P. Sartre, *Search for a Method*, translated by H. Barnes, New York, 1968, Chapters 3 and 4. For

scarcity and socialism see H.M Enzensberger, 'Critique of Political Ecology' in *Raids and Reconstructions*, London, 1976.

12 W. Reich, *Mass Psychology of Fascism*, translated by V.R. Carfagno, New York, 1970, p. 105.

13 H. Marcuse, from an interview with B. Magee whose text can be found in *The Listener*, 9 February, 1978, p. 171.

14 M. Foucault, *The History of Sexuality*, translated by R. Hurley, Harmondsworth, 1981, p. 7. Foucault's work was first published as *La Volonté de Savoir*, Paris, 1976.

15 Ibid., p. 20.

16 Ibid., p. 23.

17 Ibid., p. 105.

18 Ibid., p. 107.

19 Ibid., pp. 105-106.

20 Ibid., p. 155.

21 Ibid., p. 93.

22 Ibid., p. 103.

23 Ibid., p. 126.

24 There are numerous examples here, see, e.g. B. Stoker, *Dracula*, G. Eliot, *Middlemarch*, for predatory aristocrats or representatives of the ancien régime; for the working class see Dickens, *Oliver Twist, Dombey and Son*, and for Burke's fears of popular excess, see *Reflections on the Revolution in France*.

25 Foucault, op. cit., p. 130.

26 Ibid., p. 138.

27 Ibid., p. 136.

28 Ibid., p. 136.

29 Ibid., p. 86.

30 Ibid., p. 101. My exposition of Foucault's conception of power is not intended as an unequivocal endorsement of it. It does, however, oblige us to rethink the operations of power in relation to the traditional class/economic determinations.

31 Ibid., p. 60.

32 Ibid., p. 157.

33 Ibid., pp. 7-8.

34 Ibid., p. 145.

35 Ibid., p. 137.

36 See M. Barrett, *Women's Oppression Today*, London, 1980 and S. Rowbotham, *Women, Resistance, and Revolution*, London, 1972.

37 In what follows I'm not arguing that repression has played no part in feminist analysis. The question is one of the relative effects within a political discourse of the two terms repression and oppression.

38 P. Anderson, *Consideration of Western Marxism*, London, 1976.

39 B. Brecht, 'The Gordian Knot', *Poems 1913-1956*, London, 1981, p. 120.

40 J. Lacan, 'A Love Letter', *Feminine Sexuality*, edited by J. Mitchell and J. Rose, translated by J. Rose, London, 1982. p. 160.

41 L. Althusser, 'Ideology and Ideological State Apparatuses' in *Lenin and*

Philosophy, London, 1977, p. 162. For examples of this mode of analysis, see J. Williamson, *Decoding Advertisements*, London, 1978 and for a non-Althusserian account, see J. Berger, *Ways of Seeing*, Harmondsworth, 1972.

42 A. Rifflet-Lemaire, *Jacques Lacan*, Brussels, 1970, p. 129.
43 J. Rose, 'Introduction-II', *Feminine Sexuality*, p. 55.

Noël Greig

The Body Electric

Of that which exists in the Soul, political freedom and
institutions of equality, and so forth, are but shadows (necessarily
thrown); and Democracy in States or Constitutions but the shadow
of that which first expresses itself in the glance of the eye or the
appearance of the skin.
    Without that first the others are of no account, and need not
further be mentioned.
Edward Carpenter, *Towards Democracy*

It must be a good half hour since I typed those words. In the
meantime I've: stared out of the window, made a pot of tea,
smoked three cigarettes and thought about a friend. To tell
truth, it's the friend who is uppermost in my mind, not this
essay, and Edward Carpenter's words on eyes and skin were
enough to bring me round to picturing a certain complexion
and a particular smile.

I am rather confused. Not about the very strong feelings of
wanting to touch and be touched, but as to why, after having
known someone for several years (though not as a close friend),
his presence and appearance should begin to have such an
effect upon my nerve-endings. There is something mysterious
in that, and alarming too, for this does not usually happen
with old acquaintances, with whom a certain kind of neutered
amiability provides a refuge from the minefields of desire. A
smile from a stranger, on the other hand, can lead me to
anxiety-free thoughts of a bedding. Then, if the negotiations of
temperament and limbs collapse, there is little more harm
done than, at worst, a temporarily bruised ego. For instance,
last summer I was sitting on a wall after a demonstration, when

an unfamiliar head turned, grinned in a way which nearly made me fall off the wall, then was lost down the street. I met that person a week later, quite by chance and that night the promise of the smile was delightfully fulfilled. He and I now have a friendship which includes, in a relaxed way, sexual intimacy, yet is not dominated by it. To reverse the procedure – to progress from friendship to sex – scares the wits out of me.

I think what I mean by the above is that the *possibility* of progress from friendship to sex – the finding of the desire for it – scares me. Maybe the admission of a sexual feeling, and the chance of its rejection, comes too close to the bone of my ego and its pride. It is easier to bear that from a stranger than from someone who knows me. Yet – and here is the mysterious bit – in the case of my friend I'm not even sure what it *is* I want. With the stranger, the connection between smile and sex seems, if not inevitable, certainly uncomplicated. Somehow though, there is a different pitch to what I am feeling at the moment – the collapse of all the erotic responses into an erection and an orgasm, the urge towards that, does not feel so pressing. On the horizon of possibilities, yes, yet what I feel does not centre on that – it is more of a rather hazy, general, eroticised enjoyment of being in his company.

Now I start to embarrass myself – a sudden flash of how this may be no more than an intellectual translation of Barbara Cartland (... his presence caused the colour of rose-petals to rise to her cheeks, reflecting the same delicate colour of the chiffon which masked her tremulous bosom et cetera'). No, it's not the same, for a Ms Cartland conclusion would be marriage, whereas this might not even be about bed – or at least the erotic feelings don't seem to depend on that possibility for their existence.

I feel better for having just written that. Writing can be some kind of a therapy, a space in life to try and tease out what I'm really feeling (fascinating for me, sheer tedium for you who do not know me? – well the book is dealing with 'the erotic' and as I'm sitting here feeling it, it did seem an appropriate way to start). It's about 'the left', too, and that's why I opened with the Edward Carpenter quote. Carpenter has been a significant influence on me. He was part of a movement of late nineteenth

century socialists who were in the tradition of Robert Owen
and Mary Wollstonecraft. Utopian socialists. He was
homosexual, and came out in the movement as such, and in his
writings I have found expressions of a type of politics which
barely exists today – where the great movements of the masses
have their place, but do not diminish the individual desire or
need. Indeed, they are seen to depend on those individual
motions for their meaning and purpose. In the end Carpenter
was marginalised by the 'municipal socialists' who came to
represent the cause of Labour in parliament, but not before he
had written, spoken and lived much in the cause of (to quote
the introduction to this book) the 'possible connections
between desires, fantasies, pleasures and the kinds of
transformations in social relations which socialist convictions
involve pursuing'.

Strongly influenced by anarchist philosophies he firmly
believed that any system of society should be based upon the
uniqueness of every single individual within it, and his long
poem *Towards Democracy*, in which these ideas were embodied,
became a kind of bible for early twentieth century socialists. I
wonder how many of today's politicians and politicos could
even *begin* to start to think around the proposition that a tiny
movement of desire between two individuals, has as much to
say about the world as production-quotas, agendas and
programmes? I shall not be going into the story of how
Edward Carpenter came to be shouldered aside – it is well
documented elsewhere – though I will say that it is the same
shoddy old tale of how the feminist principle has been rejected,
trivialised and incorporated by the politics of both left and
right, all in the cause of maintaining a gender-system based
upon a sexual division of labour, rights and privileges.[1]

Perhaps I'd better talk around the matter of the
gender-system. That it centres around (in many guises) the
male desire to dominate the female is apparent – unless women
have elected over the ages to be the subject of rape,
foot-binding, low pay, no pay, purdah, wife-beating et cetera.
In this essay I shall be concentrating on the gender-system, but
would like to make it very clear that I am not saying it is *the*
division of the world which, if overcome, would bring about

the utopia. The divisions of the class-system, the divisions of racism, the division of rich North from starving South, the division of all classes and all races from nature, these are all aspects of a world set against itself. Nor do I believe that any of *these*, once settled, would lead the way to a healing of all the others. What I do believe is that there has to be a convergence of all of these towards the great healing, a type of politics in which, to dwell on one aspect of the world is not to deny all other aspects, rather an attempt to understand them.

This will be difficult, for *opposition* is generally the spirit in which we go about our business – as nations, business operations, political organizers, freelance writers, theorists, job-seekers, love-seekers. Opposition is not a bad thing, if it can effect change for the better, and the Marxist dialectic has been a very useful tool in helping us understand how that works in history. Yet a limited tool, for somewhere along the line, there must be a view of the world which sees beyond opposition, and orthodox Marxism cannot supply this. As a much fuller discussion of this elsewhere puts it:

> ... the fundamental refusal of orthodox Marxism to acknowledge the utopian dimension of communist thought derives from the contradiction between the ethical ideals at work in utopianism and the needs of violent revolution.[2]

I say 'beyond opposition' not in the sense of removing it from our common practice, but for it to have it's proper place. Today's slogans take up the themes of 'Fight' this, 'Smash' that, and maybe even necessarily so at times (I'm not a pacifist in the sense that I would allow an army to trample on my head). Yet a politics of convergence would have to recognise that beyond the symbolic rallying-call of 'Smash The ...' are human limbs and that to smash through those fragile barriers in order to reach the utopia means that we would traipse a red stickiness right across the green landscape we desire.

Where can we find a common gateway into this politics of convergence? I believe it is through a discussion of the gender-system. We may not all of us be working-class, we may not all be black, we may not all be Irish. We all of us have gender and the footsteps of all are dogged by a system which elevates the masculine practice of domination and degrades the feminist principle of reconciliation. We all pass through this gate and we all have our own stories to tell. Out of those stories perhaps we can begin to see common threads of experience which will lead us to a view of the world which centres on our common humanity.

Certainly for myself, the feminist movement and the gay movement for which it paved the way have been the nearest things to a truly internationalist movement in my lifetime (though perhaps the peace movement – which incorporates an understanding of the gender-system with its demand to 'take the toys from the boys' – has begun to take us further in that direction). I say truly internationalist not because other groups and parties have not spoken internationalism (spouted may be the best word in some cases), but because the movements opposing the gender-system quite specifically have touched on something common to all, transcending the gulfs of culture, age, race and class.

I imagine that rape means much the same thing to any woman in any part of the world, of whatever distinction of class or race. So too for the gay man who is queer-bashed, be it in Moscow or Manilla. There is a convergence of experience borne out of this system, linking the young Arab woman whose clitoris is forcibly removed and the woman in the English city afraid to go out after dark. So too – for the gender-system cripples even those who seem to benefit from it – the strands exist between the gentle Marxist writer whose anonymous wife/secretary types up his works and the Turkish peasant who sits in the cafe over cards while his wife/servant toils in the fields. They are joined together in a collusion which seems to benefit, yet ultimately lessens, them. Yes, the degrees of pain and privilege doled out by the gender-system are mediated everywhere by factors of class, race, custom and economy, but they can never be fully explained by any of these other divisions. On the other hand, to understand the gender-system might just give us a common vantage-point, the beginnings of a shared political language, taking its root not from opposing theories of the world but individual dreams and desires, fears and fantasies.

As I have said, I think theory has its use, yet I also distrust it.

When I began this essay I made a pact with myself to steer as far away from theorising as possible. In the company of friends I can cobble together theories till the cows come home, happy in the knowledge that they will let me show off as we hit the third bottle of wine, and won't sneer at my stupidities as I hog the fourth. When it comes to putting down in print, to be read by strangers, some attempt at suggesting underlying causes, I get edgy. This is something to do with what I call the 'Moses Syndrome': to log something up, print it, publish it and send it out into the world casts up the image of the Prophet coming down the mountain with the words of another man, called God, carved on tablets of rock. I have a dislike of knowledge and experience being *fixed*, and recognise that the authority of the printed word can encourage us to say 'That's it! I've seen the light!'. I'd personally rather take Edward Carpenter's advice:

> ... the fall of a leaf through the air and the greeting of one that passed on the road shall be more to you than the wisdom of all the books ever written – and of this book.[3]

So if I detour into theory I'd like to say that I'm not doing it for your benefit, though I'll be happy if what I have to say rings some bells for you. If anything I'm using this essay for one purpose – self-therapy. I'd better explain that, and maybe it will shed some light on the subject in hand. It will have to start with a bit of autobiography.

I am nearing the end of my thirties. My political education came through the movements of the sixties. I have opted for a life which is economically insecure yet creatively rewarding. I live in a licensed squat with some other gay men and a couple of cats. I was able to jump out of the working class trap I was born into, thanks to the educational advantages of having been born in 1944 (I was one of the first on our estate to get to university), and the determination of a mother who wanted me to have a broader experience of life than she ever had. My adolescent feelings of inferiority – which stemmed from the knowledge that I was 'queer' – I converted, in my sixth-form days, into a facility to be 'best' at everything (this has ended up as a tendency to show myself to the world as much more self-assured and in control than I actually often feel). In a sexually-competitive world I've had the advantage of possessing reasonable good looks.

It is now summer 1983. I am experiencing certain anxieties. I know that I shall soon be entering early middle-age with meagre material resources and securities, at a time when the opportunities for living on the fringes of the economy narrow daily. I know that I will not have the props which were available even ten years ago, when I was entering my thirties. At that time, the gradual decay of health and good looks were on a very distant horizon. Then, radical creative work within a capitalist economy on the decline did not seem such an uphill slog – due partly to the invigorating sense of being part of some broad, progressive movement, which embraced gender and class, music, political activism, love and revolt. There was that sense of 'convergence', the feeling that great changes were to happen, and that I was part of that movement. Well, things are very different now and I feel a pressing need to sift through my past years, to find those things within me that will carry me through the next patch of my life: to recognise those things around me which reflect those feelings and show me that I am not condemned to hunt around for a comfy niche in the academic establishment and write about what was and could have been.

At the moment my anxieties have not shaped themselves into such great insecurities that I am thumbing the *Guardian* jobs-pages for cosy bolt-holes. There is the Past still, the knowledge that our efforts are not isolated in time. The Present, too, grim as it is, brings forth the Great Refusal (words of Marcuse, whose writing I once ferreted through in search of 'the answer', but even so is still a good read): the Greenham Common women, the riots in Brixton and Toxteth, workers at a plant refusing to make nuclear components, environmentalists in Tasmania placing their bodies against a dam which will destroy another part of Nature, a Falklands ex-soldier bearing a placard accusing the Tories – whose war he fought – for his state of unemployment, guerrilla fighters in Latin America. And finally, the Future demanding that a new type of politics emerges. For if it does not, if the oppositional factor continues to be the motor there will *be* no future. The right recognises fully that their victory will be achieved by destroying the opponent. The destruction of the opponent has often been the means by which the left has approached its goal. That is not enough. If we are to rediscover the utopian, ethical, *moral* aspects of communism then we must begin to talk (and take action) not just around our different oppressions, but our shared humanity. I come back to the gender-system.

Around 1968 (the Paris riots, Grosvenor Square, the anti-draft movement) there was a popular slogan – 'People who talk of changing the world without changing themselves, speak with a corpse in their mouth'. I think of that, and am sure that it was not trivial to begin this essay by talking about what I am feeling for my friend. For the crux of that matter is that, whatever the outcome there, I have had to seriously think about my feelings – my erotic feelings – and whether whole portions of them, which might seem 'natural' and the essential 'Me', have in fact been shaped up by this society. Is the ease of de-emotionalised sex, and the fear of sexualised friendship 'Me'? Do I want it to be? The answer to that is No, and it is crucial to me to say it, for if 'I' can continue to change, not just react to the outer world, it is in the area of my gender. On a wider basis too, it is in this area that men can perhaps begin to contribute to a politics of convergence, by raising the problems which the notion of masculinity has created for the world. How do we do this?

Some of us made a start by defining ourselves as men who were gay. To 'come out' was to challenge the gender-system, to identify a heterosexist culture which quite literally killed us (the list of close acquaintances and friends who have committed suicide now stands as about ten and if I were to add people I knew only slightly it would be greater). To 'come out' was to make public and proud that which had been relegated to the 'private' – our own desires. Yet now, I can no longer argue for an autonomous gay movement based mainly on a shared sexuality. I go to the clubs, back-rooms and saunas, I read glossy gay publications, watch plays about gay relationships between well-heeled men, and I see how the Great Sponge of

Capitalism has soaked up the desire for the freedom of our bodies, sold it back to us in flashy, expensive clubs, clothes and package holidays. Nor am I overkeen on the parts of the gay movement which edge away from autonomy, for I see the more grudging Lesser Sponge of the Left conceding us 'Issue' and 'Rights' status. I get no satisfaction from either Sponge – my sexuality is neither a target for an advertising campaign nor an 'issue'. Can gay men continue to organise around struggles not centrally concerned with our own sexuality, bringing to the debate our own perspective and our own demands and desires? I think we can, but only if we take a long hard look at one of the basic themes of the gay movement of the past ten years. The central slogan of this theme was '2-4-6-8: Gay Is Twice As Good As Straight'.

Old slogans – like old theories – had their uses. At the moment, for me, it becomes blindingly clear that to be gay is not to be necessarily better than anyone. We *may* have an historical advantage in that, cast out from the lies that heterosexual bonding is morally correct and social stability requires a male to dominate over a female and her children, we can point to those lies and hope that others will recognise them. As a matter of fact I thank the Earth that I am gay, to have escaped the trap of socially-approved 'marriage', of the contradictions of female-male sexual relations, of proud self-reproductions et cetera ... but *better?* In what sense? In that the snares of jealousy, possession, loneliness, lust, coupledom are easier to negotiate because I am gay? Certainly not.

Here's something – as I sit here typing this part of the essay, my lover has gone out on his own. We do not live together and in point of fact I had no desire to see anyone tonight (I just wanted to sit and think of my feelings for my friend). But my lover came round, we had a meal and then he said he wanted to go out on his own. Very neat and rational, yet I know that *he* found it difficult to acknowledge he might wish to find someone else to end the evening up with and *I* found it impossible to say that all I wished to do was to sit and think about my erotic feelings about my friend. Being gay does not make that any better or easier for me, and my heterosexual

friends, female and male, when it comes down to the
nitty-gritty, express the same confusions and contradictions
and confusions. 'Better than' may be a necessary shock-tactic
and rallying point, but if the left is not to be composed of
people who think they are 'better' (and thus worth more) then
perhaps gay men should start to see that to take a lead in a
debate is not to think that we are superior as human beings.

I don't say we must subsume ourselves, or that gay-only
activities should not take place. I am talking somewhere
around the difficult area of rejecting the gender-system, yet not
rejecting those who seem to be more embedded in it than we
are. In some sense I am a gay separatist, for in some areas of
work, loving and living I know from experience that I can grow
through being with other gay men only. I say this cautiously,
for there are other situations, friendships, et cetera which do
not provide a gay context, yet are a darned sight more helpful,
loving and supportive than the notion of drawing solidarity
from my gay brothers busy making it in the Great Sponge. If I
cannot see that the pain I feel of living in this world is not
experienced by others, then what is the use of my separatism?
Total, unyielding opposition – war – death – the reduction of
'the other' to object status.

Under the present system of society we all become objects,
whether as sets of limbs to create objects or as series of desires
which consume objects. Our outer and inner lives are
determined by the 'law' of supply and demand – to the point
where all we do and all we feel seems 'natural', because the
cars, sex-aids, TV, package-holiday, latest fashion, latest
sound, latest gadget become so densely packed around us that
we cannot see through the mesh of them. They become the
mirrors in which we see 'ourselves'. Then we are at the mercy,
completely, of the next advertising campaign, even the ones
which *seem* to be offering a liberation. In this world, to
compete for cars and jobs and status is complemented by the
competition for 'happiness', 'sex' and 'love'. We buy objects to
satisfy our material needs, we turn other people into objects to
satisfy our inner needs.

I'm sitting in the garden now, as the sun has come out at
last. There are builders next door. I look at a young man and a

sequence of mental processes reduces him from a whole, complete human being, to a cock attached to a body, someone who I could use and discard as easily as a disposable aerosol. I can be promiscuous though, and I'm not edging towards a puritanical 'Thou Shalt Not', but promiscuity does raise huge questions for me. There is no visible damage in a 'contract' between two humans to be mutual sex-objects; yet to reduce erotic contact to genitals must ultimately create certain ways of looking at each other – and I feel that capitalism, the gay movement and the male urge to achieve have all colluded in presenting that as being the ultimate. If we wish to reassemble the bits and pieces of the world around us into something that we can exist in as human beings, we'll also have to reassemble the bits and pieces of human bodies we reduce each other to – to recreate our vision of the human form. Sex will then find its true place, as a major pre-occupation no doubt, but, spreading out from a narrow, genitalised, 'achieving' base it would not be at the cost of others and our own humanity.

Sex was the great uniting factor for the gay movement, but it has led us close to the dehumanization of each other, into a mirror world of the pulp romance, of Barbara Cartland. Within the covers of her impossible romances, in the anonymous dark of our back-rooms, people do not exist for each other, but as fantasies and functions. We know the lie of the fantasy of seeking the perfect mate through marriage, and the damage that can do. What of the lie of the fantasy of seeking the perfect fuck through promiscuity? In both these forms it is the neurotic quest after 'The One', the running after love and sex which means that we cannot receive it. Again, Edward Carpenter puts it much better:

> Not by running out of yourself after it comes the love which lasts a thousand years. If to gain another's love you are untrue to yourself then you are also untrue to the person whose love you would gain.
>
> Him or her whom you seek will you never find out that way – and what pleasure you have with them will haply only end in pain.[4]

All that said, the features of my own sexual-emotional life

have often reflected the grubby old gender-system. I am thankful that I'm gay, for this has helped me recognise that the strait-jacket of 'masculinity' is not inevitable or natural. Thankful also that contact with socialist thought and action has put that denial into some sort of context. Socialist ideas and sexual longings have always been in some sort of relation to each other in my life – and in my relationships they have sometimes met to produce some spark of a notion of what sort of world I desire. I would like to talk of some of the erotic attachments I have felt towards other men on the left.

My history master at school. A lovely man with sandy hair who helped me understand that history was about a broad sweep of things, that the past is alive-and-kicking in the present, that revolt was a healthy principle. If my socialism sprang from anywhere, it was in the excitement of learning through someone I loved. I would craftily ask if I could bike round to his house of a weekend, to discuss this or that detail of some essay, but my motives were not totally academic. Still today, there is often something missing from the erotic experience which leads to clutch, grasp and grapple; something which leads back to a sharing of time and conversation with another man where the erotic-sexual feelings are generalised, where the embracing warmth of friendship and the discovery of new ideas bring a sensual quality to a discussion of even the Agricultural Revolution. What he taught me included things not on the syllabus – that if we 'learn through experience', the experience of learning should engage all our senses. The connections I feel with the past, the ways history moves in and around me, are bound up with the personal connections I felt with my teacher; I cannot separate them.

Years later, another man, a lovely 'freak' who taught at a college and at the weekends would run a disco at an 'alternative' theatre-cum-social centre I had helped set up. He was a member of the CP, yet his pill-popping, music-filled life style was light years away from the stony-faced members of IS who often frequented our building. I had sort of 'come out', and I think he sort of knew it. There was certainly a sort of erotic quality to our friendship and it did not surprise me when, after several years, we did end up in bed. By that time I had indeed come out and was going to the GLF meetings in Notting Hill. It was this that led me to talk (after the bed-event) about my feelings around it – tentative perhaps, but it was certainly clear that I regarded the free exchange of sensuality between men a necessary aspect of the socialist debate. He went cold on me. As far as he was concerned, what had happened was out of time and out of history, and he made me feel that my inept attempt to explain why the GLF was important to me was out of place. His advice was that, as an actor, I should 'Join the Party and fight for that within your union'. The little dream of 'comradely love' which had begun with my history teacher fell to earth with an almighty bump.

Around that time too (early 70s) there were the men with long hair who looked like the Who and combined a new kind of male sexiness with the new 'alternative' radical politics. It took me some time to realise that their laid-back reactions to my sexuality were just as rigid as those of my CP friend's. A speech in a play which I co-authored sums up my feelings of that time.

I would like to quote it, for I suspect it connects with the experience of other gay men:

> I reckoned it was great then, when all the blokes started sitting cross-legged on cushions. Didn't half make your back ache. All long hair and acting gentle. Lovely. Well … they didn't actually *say* they didn't like queers but if I made the mistake of falling for one of them and if I ever told them that I loved them – they'd say that was 'cool, man' and they loved me too. 'Yeah, man. Love you too … brother'. Then they'd give me a hug and run like the wind to their 'old ladies' or 'chicks' or 'mates'. Then I wouldn't see them for a couple of days. And when we did meet again there'd be the solid brick wall of heterosexuality between us. 'See you, brother'.[5]

Well, eventually I gathered enough wits and courage to admit that hanging around heterosexual men was not only going to be frustrating and humiliating, it was also some kind of last-ditch stand of the heterosexual I was trained to be denying the homosexual I wanted to be. Since then I have occasionally got myself into dreadful tangles with heterosexual men but I don't *think* those have been the remnants of the lie that they are somehow 'better'.

Having moved into the arena of radical gay politics, the chances of erotic encounters and friendships with comrades was not only possible but, as it were, on the agenda. The gender system had been identified and we were going to demonstrate against it, on the streets and in our beds. Never before in history had there been such an open, defiant, demanding, political movement of same-sex identified people, and the mixture of debate and sexuality at those early Notting Hill meetings, Gay Days in Hyde Park, and giant dances at the Town Hall was thrilling.

That was over ten years ago but looking back I remember many encounters and relationships which did have a liberating effect – free exchanges of feeling and sensuality, unfettered by guilt, possession or jealousy. Here too, the immediate erotic content was (for me) meshed in with knowing that we were sharing more than our bodies, that we were connecting with a wider movement of ideas, thoughts and desires, in touch with the bodies of other men. If this sounds mawkish – like some sort of spiritual mass-orgy I'm sorry. I think I put it better, some years ago, in a lyric (for a play I wrote about Edward Carpenter). To be precise, I co-wrote the lyric with Walt Whitman, adding some of my words to some of his. I was unable to contact Mr Whitman to request this collaboration, and hope he did not mind:

> I sing the body electric
> I sing of the light that flows
> From the flesh of those that I love,
> I sing the body electric
> I sing of the flame that glows
> In the blood of those that I love.
> Those who defile the living
> Are the same as those who defile the dead;
> Those who corrupt their own bodies
> Conceal themselves.
> Therefore I sing the body electric
> I sing the body electric[6]

Now it took years for me to be able to admit to such feelings about other men, and many years too for them to be said in defiance of a body of political theory which reduced everything to warring mechanisms: The Class (pure in its hatred of the exploiters), Capital (pure in its relentless drive for profit) et cetera. Don't get me wrong, I think the Marxist analysis useful, but there was something that didn't quite fit: most of the men who preached it were *wrecks*, emotionally, physically or both. They wagged their fingers, they ranted, their voices were ugly, they towed along women who looked dispirited, they were drab and unjoyful. They were also heterosexual. This meant that (according to my way of regarding things then) they were right, no matter what. All the same there were still the mistrusts, which thankfully held me back from throwing my lot in with them. Occasionally one would come along who did not fit into that grim mould. Something would spark in me and I almost flirted with the loft. Precisely because none of them would have understood such a cheap gag, I did not go beyond the flirting – though I did not shy away from the broad, non-aligned activities of the late 60s and early 70s. At Grosvernor Square, Middle Earth, Shepton Mallet, performing plays for sit-ins at factories and universities, at Gay Days in Hyde Park, marching against the NF, at the Isle of Wight, I felt a movement of people who would see a new dawn.

Well, we were wrong. Margaret Thatcher and her cronies stalk the land, Lord Jingo raises his head and the Class has not revolted. Is it my fault? Should I have thrown in my lot with those grey men who spoke in Donkey-Jackets and Dialectic? If so many, many of us had not frittered away the precious time on 'alternative' culture, groupings and re-groupings that were not reliant on a centralised party, would the Revolution have happened? Who knows. Thank the Earth it didn't. Not under the leadership of those men, anyway. Why? Because, no matter how wayward, naive and impractical (*and* heterosexist) were the activities of the 'alternative', they were a darned sight more in tune with what the real motor of any revolution must be: selfishness. For that read 'No Imposed Rules', or 'Individualism' or 'Hedonism'. All those words and phrases that, in a certain interpretation relate to the immoral activities of privileged elites, but under another could mean the enjoyment of one's own sweet life on this beautiful planet, and at no cost to the freedom of anyone else. Those hectoring, finger-wagging men, denying their own beauty while talking of revolution could have nothing to offer me except a mechanical determinism – which, when I came out as gay and began to work within the GLM, told me that my sexuality and my endeavours were 'peripheral', 'bourgeois', 'anti-working class'. At best we were grudgingly given 'issue' status – discrimination by police, employers and others had to be recognised in terms of power mechanisms within capitalism. The matter of *why* we are discriminated against was dodged: it does not fit in with a strict class analysis, orthodox Marxist view of the world, which admits of no other form of basic division.

We hear from some quarters that 'homophobia' is a myth, a reactionary inclusion of 'The Class' in a form of behaviour which is purely the result of a class-divided society and which would melt away once 'The Class' came to power. Well, homophobia may be an extreme, institutionalised facet of a class-ridden society, but I do not believe one jot that once we are rid of that system, I should be free of the fear of the queer-basher. For if the brave path to the future is carved out by the finger-wagging men, then sure as hell the gender-system will remain intact, managed by men with whom I cannot be tactile, whose fear of their own femininity makes them lash out with tongue or with fist.

Now I can feel anger rising and my typewriter tap-tap is getting pretty ferocious. Talking about the left makes me feel decidedly unerotic.

Yet the left is there and I am on it. Shaky, shifty and divided as it is, it is the only raft to the future I can see. I know there are plenty of people on that raft who would gladly push me off it, who allow me on it through sufferance, who tell me that I can only remain on it if I help to build it into some grim battleship to their specifications.

Marx and Engels, when speaking of humanity used the term 'Men'. Well, we can't blame them too much for that, but I wonder what life on the raft would be like today if, instead of ending the Communist Manifesto with:

WORKING MEN OF ALL COUNTRIES, UNITE!
they had collaborated with Jesus, and said:
WORKING MEN OF ALL COUNTRIES,
LOVE ONE ANOTHER!

Edward Carpenter often spoke of the oceanic, all-embracing feelings which the sensual and the emotional can arouse. It is the reverse side of the coin which tells us that what binds us together are the chains of suffering and oppression. It is that vision of our common humanity which ultimately goes beyond the material body, the dimension of communism which begins to embrace ... I cannot find any other word than 'the spiritual'.

> Soon altogether shalt thou stop, little heart, and the beating and the pain here shall cease;
> But out of thee that life breathed into the lips of others shalt never stop nor cease.
> Through a thousand beautiful forms – so beautiful! – through the gates of a thousand hearts – emancipated freed we will pass on:
> I and my joy will surely pass on!

(Edward Carpenter: *Towards Democracy*)

References

1 *Edward Carpenter*, Chustichi Tsuzuki, Cambridge University Press, 1980: *Major Works of Edward Carpenter*, to be republished by The Gay Men's Press, 1984.
2 *The Spiral Path*, David Fernbach, The Gay Men's Press, 1981.
3 From *Towards Democracy* by Edward Carpenter.
4 'To Thine Own Self Be True', from *Towards Democracy* by Edward Carpenter.
5 *Only Connect* by Noël Greig and Drew Griffiths, BBC TV, 1979.
6 *The Dear Love of Comrades* by Noël Greig, Gay Men's Press, 1981.

Walt Whitman

I Sing the Body Electric

1

The bodies of men and women engirth me, and I engirth them,
They will not let me off nor I them till I go with them and
  respond to them and love them.

Was it dreamed whether those who corrupted their own live
  bodies could conceal themselves?
And whether those who defiled the living were as bad as they
  who defiled the dead?

2

The expression of the body of man or women balks account,
The male is perfect and that of the female is perfect.

The expression of a wellmade man appears not only in his face,
It is in his limbs and joints also ... it is curiously in the joints of
  his hips and wrists,
It is in his walk ... the carriage of his neck ... the flex of his
  waist and knees... dress does not hide him,
The strong sweet supple quality he has strikes through the
  cotton and flannel;
To see him pass conveys as much as the best poem ... perhaps
  more,
You linger to see his back and the back of his neck and
  shoulderside.

The sprawl and fulness of babes ... the bosoms and heads of
 women ... the folds of their dress ... their style as we pass in
 the street ... the contour of their shape downwards;

The swimmer naked in the swimming bath ... seen as he swims
 through the salt transparent greenshine, or lies on his back
 and rolls silently with the heave of the water;

Framers bare-armed framing a house ... hoisting the beams in
 their places ... or using the mallet and mortising-chisel,

The bending forward and backward of rowers in rowboats ...
 the horseman in his saddle;

Girls and mothers and housekeepers in all their exquisite
 offices,

The group of laborers seated at noontime with their open
 dinner-kettles, and their wives waiting,

The female soothing a child ... the farmer's daughter in the
 garden or cowyard,

The woodman rapidly swinging his axe in the woods ... the
 young fellow hoeing corn ... the sleighdriver guiding his six
 horses through the crowd,

The wrestle of wrestlers ... two apprentice-boys, quite grown,
 lusty, goodnatured, nativeborn, out on the vacant lot at
 sundown after work,

The coats vests and caps thrown down ... the embrace of love
 and resistance,

The upperhold and underhold – the hair rumpled over and
 blinding the eyes;

The march of firemen in their own costumes – the play of the
 masculine muscle through cleansetting trowsers and
 waistbands,

The slow return from the fire ... the pause when the bell strikes
 suddenly again – the listening on the alert,

The natural perfect and varied attitudes ... the bent head, the
 curved neck, the counting:

Suchlike I love ... I loosen myself and pass freely ... and am at
 the mother's breast with the little child,

And swim with the swimmer, and wrestle with wrestlers, and
 march in line with the firemen, and pause and listen and
 count.

3

I knew a man ... he was a common farmer ... he was the father
of five sons ... and in them were the fathers of sons ... and in
them were the fathers of sons.

This man was a wonderful vigor and calmness and beauty of
person;
The shape of his head, the richness and breadth of his
manners, the pale yellow and white of his hair and beard,
the immeasurable meaning of his black eyes,
These I used to go and visit him to see ... He was wise also,
He was six feet tall ... he was over eighty years old ... his sons
were massive clean bearded tanfaced and handsome,
They and his daughters loved him ... all who saw him loved
him ... they did not love him by allowance ... they loved
him with personal love;
He drank water only ... the blood showed like scarlet through
the clear brown skin of his face;
He was a frequent gunner and fisher ... he sailed his boat
himself ... he had a fine one presented to him by a
shipjoiner ... he had fowling pieces, presented to him by
men that loved him;
When he went with his five sons and many grandsons to hunt
or fish you would pick him out as the most beautiful and
vigorous of the gang,
You would wish long and long to be with him ... you would
wish to sit by him in the boat that you and he might touch
each other.

4

I have perceived that to be with those I like is enough,
To stop in company with the rest at evening is enough,
To be surrounded by beautiful curious breathing laughing
flesh is enough,
To pass among them ... to touch any one ... to rest my arm
ever so lightly round his or her neck for a moment ... what

is this then?
I do not ask any more delight ... I swim in it as in a sea.

There is something in staying close to men and women and
    looking on them and in the contact and odor of them that
    pleases the soul well,
All things please the soul, but these please the soul well.

5

This is the female form,
A divine nimbus exhales from it from head to foot,
It attracts with fierce undeniable attraction,
I am drawn by its breath as if I were no more than a helpless
    vapor ... all falls aside but myself and it,
Books, art, religion, time ... the visible and solid earth ... the
    atmosphere and the fringed clouds ... what was expected of
    heaven or feared of hell are now consumed,
Mad filaments, ungovernable shoots play out of it ... the
    response likewise ungovernable,
Hair, bosom, hips, bend of legs, negligent falling hands – all
    diffused ... mine too diffused,
Ebb stung by the flow, and flow stung by the ebb ... loveflesh
    swelling and deliciously aching,
Limitless limpid jets of love hot and enormous ... quivering
    jelly of love ... white-blow and delirious juice,
Bridegroom-night of love working surely and softly into the
    prostrate dawn,
Undulating into the willing and yielding day,
Lost in the cleave of the clasping and sweetfleshed day.

This is the nucleus ... after the child is born of woman the man
    is born of woman,
This is the bath of birth ... this is the merge of small and large
    and the outlet again.

Be not ashamed women ... your privilege encloses the rest ... it
    is the exit of the rest,
You are the gates of the body and you are the gates of the soul.

The female contains all qualities and tempers them ... she is in
  her place ... she moves with perfect balance,
She is all things duly veiled ... she is both passive and active ...
  she is to conceive daughters as well as sons and sons as well
  as daughters.

As I see my soul reflected in nature ... as I see through a mist
  one with inexpressible completeness and beauty ... see the
  bent head and arms folded over the breast ... the female I
  see,
I see the bearer of the great fruit which is immortality ... the
  good thereof is not tasted by roues, and never can be.

6

The male is not less the soul, nor more ... he too is in his place,
He too is all qualities ... he is action and power ... the flush of
  the known universe is in him,
Scorn becomes him well and appetite and defiance become
  him well,
The fiercest largest passions ... bliss that is utmost and sorrow
  that is utmost become him well ... pride is for him,
The fullspread pride of man is calming and excellent to the
  soul;
Knowledge becomes him ... he likes it always ... he brings
  everything to the test of himself,
Whatever the survey ... whatever the sea and the sail, he strikes
  soundings at last only here,
Where else does he strike soundings except here?

The man's body is sacred and the woman's body is sacred ... it
  is no matter who,
Is it a slave? Is it one of the dullfaced immigrants just landed
  on the wharf?

Each belongs here or anywhere just as much as the welloff ...
  just as much as you,
Each has his or her place in the procession.

All is a procession,
The universe is a procession with measured and beautiful
    motion.

Do you know so much that you call the slave or the dullfaced
    ignorant?
Do you suppose you have a right to a good sight ... and he or
    she has no right to a sight?
Do you think matter has cohered together from its diffused
    float, and the soil is on the surface and water runs and
    vegetation sprouts for you ... and not for him and her?

7

A slave at auction!
I help the auctioneer ... the sloven does not half know his
    business.

Gentlemen look on this curious creature,
Whatever the bids of the bidders they cannot be high enough
    for him,
For him the globe lay preparing quintillions of years without
    one animal or plant,
For him the revolving cycles truly and steadily rolled.

In that head the allbaffling brain,
In it and below it the making of the attributes of heroes.

Examine these limbs, red black or white ... they are very
    cunning in tendon and nerve;
They shall be stript that you may see them.

Exquisite senses, lifelit eyes, pluck, volition,
Flakes of breastmuscle, pliant backbone and neck, flesh not
    flabby, goodsized arms and legs,
And wonders within there yet.

Within there runs his blood ... the same old blood ... the same red running blood;

There swells and jets his heart ... There all passions and desires
... all reachings and aspirations:
Do you think they are not there because they are not expressed
in parlors and lecture-rooms?

This is not only one man ... he is the father of those who shall
be fathers in their turns,
In him the start of populous states and rich republics,
Of him countless immortal lives with countless embodiments
and enjoyments.

How do you know who shall come from the offspring of his
offspring through the centuries?
Who might you find you have come from yourself if you could
trace back through the centuries?

8

A woman at auction,
She too is not only herself ... she is the teeming mother of
mothers,
She is the bearer of them that shall grow and be mates to the
mothers.

Her daughters or their daughters' daughters ... who knows
who shall mate with them?
Who knows through the centuries what heroes may come from
them?

In them and of them natal love ... in them the divine mystery
... the same old beautiful mystery.

Have you ever loved a woman?
Your mother ... is she living? ... Have you been much with
her? and has she been much with you?
Do you not see that these are exactly the same to all in all

nations and times all over the earth?

If life and the soul are sacred the human body is sacred;
And the glory and sweet of a man is the token of manhood
    untainted,
And in man or woman a clean strong firmfibred body is
    beautiful as the most beautiful face.

Have you seen the fool that corrupted his own live body? or
    the fool that corrupted her own live body?
For they do not conceal themselves, and cannot conceal
    themselves.

Who degrades or defiles the living human body is cursed,
Who degrades or defiles the body of the dead is not more
    cursed.

Frankie Rickford

No More Sleeping Beauties And Frozen Boys

Sex is a difficult subject to write about, harder than gardening (though green lives might depend on your words) or even Thatcherism. You have to pick your way through a theoretical minefield, avoiding both voluntarism and determinism without being trapped by liberalism, and still try and say something. But worse, your own tender heart may be poked about and scorned by the reader, because however carefully you cover your tracks in arid generalisations you ultimately have only your own experience to analyse, your own loving to scrutinise and your own desires and fears to unscramble.

I begin with the proposition that 'the erotic' is a deceitful word which conceals a very complicated range of meanings and feelings behind an apparently simple name. 'The erotic' is used a bit like 'the visual', as if it was the dimension of the material world that happens to stimulate one particular human sense organ like sight, only perhaps a little more elusive. All quite natural and we-all-know-what-we-mean-by-it-don't-we. Except of course that people with the same physiology are sexually excited by quite different experiences, and even the same person can find a film, book or human being very erotic one moment and not at all some time later.

But if desire has no foundation in biology, neither does sexual pleasure. The boundary between our perceptions of erotic and non-erotic behaviour depends on the circumstances, not the activity itself, and it can shift.

A doctor examining a man for herpes, for example, might approximate the gestures made by his lover the previous midnight, but few people experience Special Clinics as dens of passion. Stroking a cat or caressing a baby over a chat in the kitchen would not usually be described as having sex, yet doing the same things to another naked adult in the middle of the night probably would be.

Another illustration of the absence of any necessary connection between sexual pleasure and any particular behaviour is rape, a profoundly non-erotic experience for the raped, characterised by terror and humiliation. Yet people still teach their children that the merging of penis and vagina is 'the sex act' – the ultimate erotic experience which every self-respecting home should have as often as possible.

Sexual intercourse, supposedly the king of the erotic castle, illustrates the contradictory way in which people's sexual self-identity is constructed by society. It is sold as being as natural as the birds and the bees – and if you don't like it there is something wrong with you. But many young people still have to undertake extensive research to discover what this natural-as-breathing business is all about, using as source material a combination of jokes, agony aunt columns, durex packets and incomprehensible diagrams of rabbits. And when they do work it all out, and when they try it, three-quarters of the girls will never in their lives experience from it the orgasm they are taught to expect. Sexual intercourse may be very pleasurable to some people with some other people, sometimes. But its elevation to a point where it and only it counts as Having Sex has wrecked our capacity to explore and choose our pleasures with whomever pleases us, including ourselves. An early 70s feminist cartoon encapsulated the sexual contradiction. 'If I get my feminine instincts naturally I'm not having you telling me how to be a woman,' said the stroppy schoolgirl.

Having argued that our sexual identity – what we desire and what we do – has to all intents and purposes no instinctive or biological basis, I will look at how the dominant erotic culture is maintained, and make some observations about less visible desires. The point of any 'political' analysis of sexuality is to inform a strategy for change, and the object of this is to suggest what might constitute progress for women, and, I believe, ultimately for men too.

Pornographic culture defines and celebrates sexuality as absolutely depersonalised. It reflects an eroticism which is knitted inextricably with contempt and self-contempt, fear, hatred and violence to self or another. As long as 'the erotic' successfully masquerades as universal and immutable, pornographers can defend anything they can get an audience for on the grounds that it coincides with human sexual desire. 'Adult' films and videos suggest they are aimed at adults in general – created with their tastes in mind just like Micky Mouse was made for children. Anyone who doesn't like them is therefore either not a real adult or is repressing his or her appetite. It is always the dissident from porn's account of sexual pleasure who is wrong, abnormal and unhealthy.

Pornographic eroticism is not an exclusively male sexuality. Men certainly consume most of it, but that may be no more significant than the fact that they consume more beer than women – they have more money, more free time and less timidity. But women 'understand' pornographic culture. Feminists (and possibly some other anti-porn campaigners) have taken up the issue of pornography not principally because the images and relations it proposes are like a foreign language to us, but because we believe we can pick and choose whole dimensions of ideology, rejecting plenty and building new ones, even though they claim a biological basis and with it invincibility.

Pornography forges and celebrates associations – in particular between subjugation and pleasure – which nourish the fear, hatred and self-hatred we have picked up along life's merry way as we've been taught to oppress and tolerate oppression.

The detail of the words and pictures – who does what to whom most often – are fairly irrelevant to the point that we know it is not what we want, not how we want our, or men's sexuality defined and propagated. If all those images of women being bound, beaten, raped, even killed by men were to be replaced by more of the others in which women assault men, I do not believe as a movement we should, or would be satisfied. But the celebration of men's violence towards women is particularly offensive because the fear of it controls and constrains women in every sphere of our lives, and the reality of it kills and maims thousands. Women and men have been created by society as victim and aggressor – and both contribute to the perpetuation of the relationship – ultimately it is we women who risk losing our lives because of it, and who have the greatest cause to end it.

However I do not believe that men in any genuine sense benefit from the violent subjugation of women, or that their initiation into masculinity can be in their interests. To become men, children are brutalised and abandoned, denied the fundamental human requirement of physical contact, loving touch, cuddles, as well as the opportunity to discharge their fear and pain in trembling tears. Masculinity may be a state of frozen terror and the urgency of men's sexual desire, a desperation to bury themselves in a warm body to escape from it for a few seconds. In any case male sexuality no more consists of a simple sadism than women's consists of a simple masochism. Mutuality and relaxed affection are perfectly possible in close relationships between women and men alongside the kind of impersonal parasitism I've described *and* the sado-masochism of pornographic erotica.

A very great deal of what both men and women experience as sexual longing might be met in a society which did not leave us so physically cut off from each other. Non-sexual physical warmth – real, sustained tender comfort as opposed to the symbolic peck or pat – is almost unavailable outside sexual relationships. Only in the context of a sexual encounter can most people uncover their skin and hold it next to someone else's, get themselves appreciatively touched and tangibly loved. Mothers of babies often describe losing interest in sex sometimes for years after a child's birth. The cuddling and closeness permissible between parents and small children leaves the mother, who generally has a lot more physical contact with the child than the father, replete. Other women – friends, aunties, grandmothers – even strangers – and some men – will do their best to cash in on babies ('Isn't she lovely – can I hold her for a minute?') because the opportunities for a good cuddle are so few and far between. It's becoming more acceptable for men to show affection to children, but many still feel it's inappropriate to be seen kissing a baby, and clearly have much less preparation for caring for children than women, most of whom are plied with dolls before they themselves can even speak. Men have little experience of expressing affection other than sexually, as they are totally physically marooned from each other even as boys.

The ferocity of the social prohibition on physical affection between men has maintained its grip over the last ten years, although relations between women, and between women and men, have changed quite dramatically among some groups. Socialist men, for example, are much less prone to lunging at women now, but show me a heterosexual man in the mainstream of the left who cuddles his brothers.

The tenacity of men's isolation from each other makes the achievements of the gay men's movement even more remarkable, although it has obviously confined its attention to explicitly sexual relationships between men. At the public service union NALGO's 1983 annual conference, held on the Isle of Man where male homosexuality is still fully criminalised, about 300 delegates, a minority of them openly lesbian or gay, marched through Douglas with the union banner to present a petition to the local legislating authority, the House of Keys. Most of the marchers had probably never been actively involved in any kind of sexual politics. Yet they faced abuse from onlookers, who clearly assumed everyone on the demonstration was gay. It seems to me to represent a remarkable advance that a trade union should stage what may have been the first ever public challenge to the island's Sexual Offences Act, and also that so many were prepared to go beyond passing pious motions and do that very frightening thing of openly marching as a group of lesbians and gay men in such a hostile place.

Relationships between and among women were a source of support and comfort, including physical comfort, long before the women's liberation movement raised the value women placed upon ourselves and each other. But. contemporary feminism has propelled thousands of women of one generation to make an irreversible commitment to womankind and radically reform their relationships with other women on the basis of solidarity and pride rather than competitiveness and shame. It has become very fashionable to rubbish the idea of sisterhood, but the fact that we do not always hear one another, or are made to feel hurt and betrayed even bored and despairing by each other, cannot outweigh the seriousness with which we take each other, especially when compared to the days when the Girl Guides, and Women's Institutes were ridiculed by women themselves *because* they were all female. Women who have had no direct contact with the feminist movement have a reference point from which to acknowledge their regard for each other and resist the jibes of frightened men who call it gossiping or bitching when women friends talk together.

But not only do we take each other more seriously, we have also discovered *en masse* the delights of women's company. We were not the first of course. Stevie Smith's Pompey in *Novel on Yellow Paper* (published in 1936), says of her friend Harriet:

> Sometimes when we are laughing together, and thinking that together it is easier and we have so very much more fun together than ever we do with our exacerbating, sulky, messiah-maniacal or crosspatchy young men, suddenly the talk will touch lightly on some subject and then up it flares and out. And sweeping up and out, it is an exultation and an agony, but so sweet it should not be missed.

 That was happening all over the place in the early 1970s, not only in people's front rooms but at meetings, conferences, in pubs and at 'socials'. Many women who had previously desired only men began to acknowledge the beauty of other women as well as how nice we were. In the context of the women's movement the boundaries between the erotic and the non-erotic shifted; we were able to perceive our pleasure in each other as desire and pursue it. The touch scent of female skin with which we were familiar through non-sexual physical closeness became sexualised – associated with the possibility of erotic pleasure. The first time I saw my mother after I began a love affair with another woman, I was embarrassed by the intimacy we had always shared. Our physical affection was suddenly wrenched out of its asexual box in my head because I had learnt to perceive similar physical tenderness with another woman as part of a sexual relationship. But when we changed the basis of our relationships with other women from 'just friends' to lovers or potential lovers, the pattern of the relationships changed too. As lovers, we became more emotionally vulnerable and felt able to express greater needs and demands.

Sometimes women become sexually involved with each other because it seemed to be the only way to say, 'I like you and want to get close to you,' and to exchange a commitment to see each other regularly, without the time consuming business of becoming Old Friends. What is experienced as sexual desire is the same sort of enthusiasm about another person that when we were schoolgirls caused us to exchange a drop of blood or solemnly ask, 'Will you be my best friends?' The lesbian feminist movement within women's liberation created its own erotic culture to which friendship and sisterhood were integral. At least outside London, heterosexual women too could share what was going on, a flirt, dance and cuddle in the generally unpredatory atmosphere of feminist bops.

Of course life wasn't always a bed of roses. We had changed, but still dragged fears and insecurities frozen in the depths of infancy around with us, which women were no better able to assuage than men, though they were usually less panic stricken by being presented with emotional demands. Sometimes the disappointment of discovering that lesbianism, which was and is seen by many feminists as a political solution to the problem of men, could be just as bitter and painful and debilitating as heterosexuality, was devastating. I believe that one of the greatest difficulties the women's movement confronts, which may eventually destroy it in its present 'phase', is the demoralisation and cynicism directly attributable to that disappointment, and the damage it has done to women's solidarity. Some feminists who have always and only desired women were distrustful of those of us who 'turned' during those years and undoubtedly feel angry and betrayed by the many who now have male lovers again.

Lesbian women still face the most crushing social contempt and disgust because they pose such a direct challenge to an order which assumes the interdependence of men and women in a relationship of relative power and powerlessness. If women claim they can survive or worse, thrive, without having to put up with men's institutionalised emotional and domestic leeching, then, by god, society will do its very best to prove them wrong.

It is terrifying to be a member of a despised and persecuted minority, to risk losing your children, to bewilder your family, to embarrass your colleagues at work, to be ignored or sneered at in pubs and restaurants and face violent assault if you dare touch in public in ways that heterosexual lovers don't think twice about. The first time I went out with a male lover after four years as a lesbian I remember basking in this almost palpable glow of social approval as we sat together on the bus. My status suddenly shot up; I was an associate Someone, and compared to being a No-one it was glorious. and to be able to introduce a man to my parents, whom I love, and prove I cared enough about them to be *like* them, was sweet indeed.

So let it be acknowledged that some women, including me, found the going hard as lesbians. But it was also true that I found men more likeable than ever before because I was less frightened of them, more sure of who I was and what I wanted, and more prepared to say what was and what was not acceptable. In that sense, the re-entry into heterosexuality represented an assertion that I could take charge of my relationship to men, even though we entered it on unequal terms. To desire men, and actually to desire women too, has to mean being quite clear about the detailed content of the relationship you want, and go for it, rather than tiptoeing around responding to the other's initiatives. Responsiveness is after all what characterises feminine sexuality. From Sleeping Beauty to *Playboy*'s waiting Playmate, we were brought up to react, to comply or complain but never actually take the reins and calmly make happen what we want. The very question, 'What do I want?' is confounding if it has never before been seriously suggested that you have the power to control your own futures, in terms of sex or anything else. The core demand of the women's liberation movement, a woman's right to determine her own sexuality, *does* make the point. But to kick away enough of the consequences of oppression to make that possible is a goal for ourselves rather than a demand of anyone else.

Zelda Curtis

'Private' Lives and Communism

'I've had enough of these middle-class, middle-aged Romeos.' The young comrade flung these words at me, even as she flung her Party card on the table and walked out of the room. I was left wondering how to explain her resignation to the other comrades, mostly male. I knew the sexual criticism would be ignored, that no concern would be felt, let alone expressed, at their now obvious sexual abuse of a woman comrade. The open expression of her anger would be ignored, even as the covert sexual advances had been known of and ignored previously. Discussing with another woman comrade what action to take, my thoughts were confirmed. She assured me that it wasn't the *real* reason the comrade had resigned, but just an excuse. After all, she had been complaining for a long time about our attitudes to the ETU ballot-rigging episode. Her words were confirmed when the resignation was announced. 'it was to be expected,' said the others. The ex-comrade was 'immature', 'lacked political understanding', 'an hysterical character', 'impressionable'. Words too often used even today to describe women's behaviour.

Closing one's eyes to comrades' sexual relations and sexual practices had long been the norm. Keeping one's mouth closed about them was even more necessary, as a good public image of the Party had to be maintained. Not that we ever discussed whether we should or shouldn't. There was a 'moral' climate, an expectation of behaviour that was prevalent, not just in the Party but in the movement as a whole.

Of course, that didn't mean there was any restriction on one's sexual practices or relationships, just that people looked the other way, never openly discussed them or were terribly careful not to bring 'disgrace' on the movement. Any fear of that and you did get a leading comrade having words with you!

Now that I look back on those times from the present feminist perspective, I feel tremendous anger: anger directed at myself, the Party, and the movement as a whole, for the damage we allowed to be done – in particular to women, lesbians and homosexuals, but indeed to all individual human beings, let alone the collective good, by ignoring the personal. And yet it was the collective good we thought we were protecting. The individual good was submitted to it.

Strange that I, who had moved to the left through my hatred of hypocrisy, should stomach it so readily within the left, and accept from such hypocrites a burden of guilt for my own seeming shortcomings.

At sixteen, through attending WEA Classes and discussions led by a Communist, my eyes had been opened to the vision of a socialist world in which people would be able to develop to their full potential. That full potential, I now realise in hindsight, only applied to intellect, artistic talents and work potential – nobody ever mentioned sexuality. The mind boggles when one thinks of trying to assess the merits and demerits of clitoral or vaginal stimulation in the climate of that period!

Lillian Hellman described the Russians of that period as 'romantic and dawn-fogged about sex'. Perhaps with my then burgeoning sexuality hot upon me, I may have felt that the development of the full sexual potentiality of women, freed of unequal power relationships, was implicit in socialism. Yet, how odd that those comrades, so concerned for my development, should never point me toward Alexandra Kollontai's pamphlet *Communism and the Family*, published in 1920, in which she was arguing that the

> old type of family has seen its day ... we shall soon behold rising a new form which will involve altogether a different relationship between men and women, and which will be a union of affection and comradeships, a union of two equal persons of the communist society, both of them free, both of them independent, both of them workers.

No, I had to wait until recently to read that! They only reiterated Lenin's rebukes to women comrades 'inclined to support and praise superficial sexual relations' (from a Soviet booklet *Marriage and the Family in the USSR*) and that oft-repeated quote, that encapsulates Lenin's feelings about 'love as a glass of water', namely 'who would wish to drink from a cracked glass?' I think I might agree with Lillian Hellman when she said she found in Russia 'the talk about love and fidelity too high-minded for my history or my taste'.

But my hopes for the flowering of a new improved model of people under socialism continued, though I am very sad now when I read again words like those of Oscar Wilde describing the 'true personality of man' which will be seen under socialism:

It will grow naturally and simply ... It will know everything. And yet it will not busy itself about knowledge. It will have wisdom. Its value will not be measured by material things ... It will *not always be meddling with others or asking them to be like itself. It will love them because they will be different.* (My italics).

He said that 'Know Thyself' was written over the portals of the ancient world, but over the new world 'Be Thyself' shall be written. To 'know thyself' is the first step to 'being thyself' in my opinion, yet did we ever in discussion on the left from the end of the thirties onwards ever really try to delve into the personal? I can only speak from my own experience, and perhaps I was unlucky, but I can only answer 'No'.

I can remember some perfunctory discussions among comrades in the late forties and fifties on Freud – but he was always dismissed. 'Nature or nurture', heredity or environment, was often discussed in the most learned of terms. To the Party environment was all. I used to have great difficulty with Party sympathisers, to whom I was trying to sell literature, and who would snap at me 'dogmatist'.

That was the time, too, of the controversy around Lysenko's theories and their implication for human evolution. Lysenko looked outside the organism for the factors directly affecting its heredity and found them in the environment. His experiments on plants were decried in the capitalist press and hugely praised in the Soviet journals we saw in this country. The Party followed suit, but there was controversy raging in the *Daily Worker* and other Party journals, with hard-hitting articles by Professor Haldane condemning a dogmatic approach. Later Lysenko fell into disgrace in the Soviet Union when his experiments failed.

We also read and discussed the bestselling Soviet books of the time, those of the Soviet educationalist Makarenko, *A Book for Parents* and *The Road to Life*, on the development of the child. The Russian Dr Spock! He never used a cane, only encouraged with the 'carrot' of incentive. He told the parents to 'be with the child, talk to him, do things with him' and if still the child was a disappointment to the parents then they should look into themselves and ask 'Have I in my family life acted like a Bolshevik?' How we lapped it up! Against competitiveness and greed, he said 'greed is refuelled by capitalism. In human desire there is no greed'. His example of a perfect family was one with 13 children where there was 'no sadness' despite their hard life and where they took decisions on a collective basis. Each had their place in the structure of the family, each their own tasks, but all was for the collective good. No place for individualism.

When I first joined the Party I was performing at Unity Theatre, and long into the night after the show we would discuss that 'new man' who would develop during the struggle for socialism and come to full flowering after 'the withering of the State'. We would also argue about art for art's sake or commitment to the revolution, would talk of nihilism, thrash out Lenin's ideas on 'infantile disorders', anguish over the political questions of the day, but sexuality was never on the official agenda. But in the bar at Unity it was boasted that one comrade 'had been through every woman in the show's cast'. I was later to learn he was impotent, though his conversations were pregnant with sexual images.

Remembering the many lesbian and homosexual friends I had at Unity, some in the Party but many not, I asked a Labour Party friend if she remembered any discussions on sexuality or any particular attitudes towards it on the left at that time. 'One didn't talk about such things' she said. 'Except to one's friends, of course'. What people did in their sex lives was their business. But I remember one of our mutual friends, a homosexual feeling desperately unhappy at the break-up of a long-term relationship. His partner had met a woman who had encouraged him to 'seek help for his *condition*' through psychiatry. Then, 'cured', he had settled down with her. Our friend, in his desperation, had also been persuaded to visit a psychiatrist. One afternoon when a number of friends were sitting chatting over coffee, he burst in announcing with a laugh, 'Darlings, isn't it wonderful, he can't do a thing for me. Whoopee!'

Rehearsal rooms at that time were in Little Newport Street and many of us would go on from there to the 'gay bars' of the time, the *French House* or *The Salisbury* and then on for a snack at Coffee Ann which was open practically all night except when raided by the Military Police, as often occurred. There we'd discuss every political question, but never the lifestyle questions that were around us, the personal ones.

Recently I asked a comrade active in the Party much earlier than I had been whether there had been discussions about personal relationships and sexuality in her period. 'Of course not, we were all much too busy.' Every hour was organised – so much so that there was even a question raised at Committee level as to whether she should be allowed to visit her aunt on a Friday night when there was so much to be done. 'Personal relationships' – what were they? But what about sexuality, I pressed, did you ever on your reading days (yes, they had them) discuss Freud, Havelock Ellis or any such writers. 'Well, Freud was disapproved of, of course, but anyway we were too preoccupied with the works of Stalin or Lenin's *What Is To Be Done?*' was her response. 'What about practice?' I persevered. Everyone knew who was homosexual or hetero, and who was having a relationship with whom, but it was never discussed. Closed eyes again. A moral public image was all. The personal was private.

Just as an interesting aside: one leading comrade of her time used publicly to *apologise* for having 'married' his wife. 'Should never have done it' ... 'bourgeois'. The fact that his wife was having personal problems didn't apparently impinge on the consciousness of the other comrades, let alone take up their time or energy to give her some support.

As for the 'moral public image', where did that spring from, I asked. It was a development of the United Front, worked for and won in the thirties, I was told. One was expected to set a good example, to dress inconspicuously (away with the sandals and open shirt image beloved of the intellectual – trade unionists put on their best clothes to go to union meetings) and certainly one should be 'the best' at anything one attempted, especially better than any non-political person. And all to the honour of 'Uncle Joe', a prime example of all that was good. (Until the revelations of Svetlana Alliluyeva, one didn't know how many times that good man had been married, or what child came from what woman, nor what had happened to those women.) Some women in the Party knew their place only too well. One such said she knew her role in the Party was to make sure her husband, a leading comrade, was best able to perform his Party responsibilities. She made sure, she said, he had good hot meals and clean clothing. (And that's on tape for posterity!) Each had their place in the scheme. The whole would show the world how much better a socialist society could be.

The 'moral public image' as a means of best propaganda for militants is not dead – in an interview on TV recently I heard a man taking part in the People's March for Jobs say: 'We're very conscious that we have to reflect the best morality'. And the 'best morality' was preached at us from many publications.

In a Syllabus of the Party's Education Department called *Women's Place in Society*, we were told that

> Equality and greater freedom to marry and divorce does not mean irresponsibility. Lenin was very definite on this. He said 'In love two lives are concerned and a third, a new life arises. It is this which gives it its social interest, which gives rise to a duty toward the community.' ... It is only under Socialist Society that true happiness and dignity in marriage and family life are possible ... In Soviet society, people not property or profits, are regarded as the most precious asset of the country. That is why motherhood

and large families are held in high regard and the care of mothers and children is a first charge on the Soviet State. The work of mothers in bringing up young citizens is regarded as a noble task and is honoured by the Order of Maternal Glory, the Maternal Medal and the title Mother Heroine which are conferred on Soviet women. With these awards go special grants of money.

The Party women's journal of the late 1940s and early 1950s was *Woman Today*, devoted mainly to the issues of peace and struggle for better childcare facilities to enable women to work outside the home. It did, however, find space to discuss some personal issues, though usually in the letters columns.

In its 'agony' column of the October 1946 issue, this letter appeared:

> My wife and I were apart for five years. I was prepared to find her altered, but she is different in so many ways. I can't *get up* any feeling of affection for her. We were happy before the war. Is there any way of going back? (my italics)

The answer:

> Recognise that during the war your wife gained a new and valuable independence – stop resenting the fact she is not the same.

No word of any sexual difficulties that might be bugging them, as appears to me to be implicit in what he's saying. So many women, freed from home and family restrictions by the war, had encountered different sexual experiences, had broadened their sexual horizons, and that had created difficulties for returning husbands.

Though I didn't find much on sexual relationships in *Women Today*, on a quick re-reading of some old copies, some quotes from the magazine might interest you.

In September 1947 in an article on 'The Growing up Years', it was said that a 'young girl needs to be beautiful in her own right, it is part of her equipment as she turns to the world wanting to be liked'. And in February 1947, discussing a current wireless programme that brought married couples to

the mike to discuss their problems, the journal said 'What is
the same for most married couples is the day-to-day struggle
to keep to a certain standard of living. When things change and
improve, then people's reactions to each other will improve'.

There was an unusual discussion on the menopause in later
years. In a letter in November 1956, they stated that 'social
conditions play an important part. The happily married
woman is more likely to pass easily through the menopause
than the lonely woman who faces an insecure old age'. A reply
suggested 'menopause clinics' as an answer. That elicited this
sarcastic response in January 1957:

> We notice one of your expert's ideas put forward in the form of a
> political demand at the end of the article suggests that women
> should 'demand through your organisations menopause clinics in
> every town'! We think this demand really doesn't go far enough
> and we should really be putting forward a more ambitious
> demand which would lead to 'Total abolition of the menopause
> under a people's government'. Just how silly can one get?

By October 1957, in an atmosphere of heightened awareness of
the nuclear threat, a man wrote, in answer to a mother who
was concerned about sexual maniacs and what she should say
to her young daughter, 'if we get rid of the threat of nuclear
war we could get rid of the fear that drives these poor wretches
insane'.

In February 1958, prostitution was on the agenda. It was
said that there were 'many ways in which a woman acquires the
psychological make-up for prostitution in capitalist society,
quite apart from the effects of entertainment of a suggestive
character, dubious ads, sale of pornography, drugs, alcohol,
etc.,' and they were concerned that the Wolfenden Committee
report had no recommendations that 'attempt to abolish
prostitution or make prostitution itself illegal'.

The Party submitted a proposal that following a conviction
for the use of premises as a brothel, the premises should 'be
requisitioned and made available for rehousing those on
waiting lists'. In this context it is interesting to remember
Alexandra Kollontai's thoughts on prostitution, that

after marriage has given place to the free and honest union of men and women who are lovers and comrades, another scourge will also be seen to disappear, another frightful evil which is a stain on humanity and which falls with all its weight on the hungry working women – prostitution.

Woman Today ceased publication not long after and we were not to see sexuality fully discussed in our journals again until *Red Rag* leapt into the fray. But in the intervening years I was working for the *Morning Star*. As Fund Organiser I received thousands of letters during a month. The warmth and generosity of the comrades was tremendous, and their commitment total. It was a wonderful experience for me. But some of those correspondents, and only a few let me reassure you, let their letters spill over into the personal and sexual realities. Oh, the unhappy lives. But also, and to me so extraordinary coming from some I knew to be so outwardly morally pure, some outpourings of sexual abuse that were hard to take.

My work also sent me out of London to meet with people in the labour movement throughout Britain, and I learned a great deal of the attitudes prevailing in the movement, attitudes that did not always match up with their progressive stance.

I remember my shock when I went to speak to a Miners' Lodge meeting in a Working Men's Club. Firstly, I wasn't let into the actual meeting upstairs as I had expected, but was taken down to talk with 'the lads' over a drink in a corner of the club while at the other end a strip show was being leered at! And that was on a Sunday lunchtime! Naturally, I was expected to take it all with 'humour' and 'good grace'. But, how often, too, I was shocked by trade unionists' venom toward gays and lesbians. For their macho image to remain untarnished they had to be seen to be anti-gay – and what a threat to them lesbians were.

During this time I also had the opportunity to see some of the socialist countries and discover whether attitudes had changed there. Certainly not as regards women ... Equal opportunity? Just go and see the carnation nursery I saw in

Romania where the low-paid back-breaking work was done by women and the supervisors were men in white coats, or the carpet factory where most of the overseers were men. Control of their own bodies? Women in the Soviet Union and other socialist countries were sadly jealous of our freedom to have the contraceptive pill. Their fertility was controlled by abortion. Violence against women? I saw a fight in a side street in Moscow between a man and his wife – the onlookers urging him on.

Yet still I saw, both in Moscow and Bucharest, women going eagerly into marriage. A Hungarian comrade confided in me that he was terribly unhappy about his daughter of sixteen getting married. He knew she was only doing it because of the cramped conditons in which they lived as a family. No, socialism hasn't yet brought the answers for us.

But I was not without hope, for by then we were seeing an influx of young recruits into the Party bringing new vigour, new ideas and new hopes for comrades like me. And with what relief did I welcome the new freer climate of discussion of the personal that came in their wake. But new ideas take time to take hold of even the minds of progressives, let alone actually change their attitudes. That 'freer climate of discussion' did not to start with bring with it a greater tolerance or sensitivity among comrades. How many meetings I sat through where anger exploded, where comrades' views were derided and even, on occasions, where people were verbally abused. Gradually, however, as many of us felt greater confidence in speaking out, gained through the tremendous support of the wider women's movement, the attitudes of both men and women comrades began to change – in their spoken theories if not yet in practice.

What worries me now is that while so many on the left have taken on board feminist ideas and grappled with problems of sexuality, the climate now is beginning to change yet again. At the very time of greatest backlash from Thatcher and Co., with their return to Victorian morality, the personal is beginning to take a back seat again in the left's political arena.

Michael Eaton

Lie Back and Think of England

Power is essentially what dictates its law to sex. Which means first of all that sex is placed by power in a binary system: licit and illicit, permitted and forbidden. Secondly, power prescribes an 'order' for sex that operates at the same time as a form of intelligibility: sex is to be deciphered on the basis of its relation to law. And, finally, power acts by laying down the rule: power's hold on sex is maintained through language, or rather through the act of discourse that creates, from the very fact that it is articulated, a rule of law.

Michel Foucault – *The History of Sexuality*

There is a Victorian joke which, whilst you might not find it particularly comic, is nevertheless of more than antiquarian interest. In a state of some anxiety, a Victorian lady summoned the family physician to procure his assistance in securing committal proceedings against her son. The doctor, not unnaturally, asked her for evidence of his behaviour which might lend support to the drastic assertion that the fruit of her womb was indeed insane.

'Well,' said the lady, 'last year, at Christmas time, he would creep downstairs in the middle of the night and eat up all the mince pies.'

'That is only gluttony, madame,' says the medical man, 'I'm afraid we shall need a little more evidence than that.'

'There is something else,' said the mother, 'but it is of such a delicate nature that I shrink from telling you ... nevertheless, I arrived home yesterday to find him in the act of debauching the housemaid on the back stairs.'

'Depravity, madame, mere depravity. Nothing in what you

say convinces me of his madness,' said the doctor who was a plain speaking man, 'now, if we'd have caught him eating the servant and fucking the mince pies we might have some cause for confining him in a lunatic asylum.'[1]

This joke is, structurally, not very sophisticated, based as it is on a simple linguistic transposition of verb and object. However, its narrative contains four of the most common dramitis personae in the High Victorian Passion Play: the repressive Mother; the perverse and rapacious young man; the seduced servant, and the doctor whose professional discourse of sickness and health, sanity and madness, articulates and justifies behaviour.

Anyone who has read Wilkie Collins' classic novel of detection *The Moonstone*, may recognise it as something of a structural transposition of the joke. For the central enigma of that story concerns a young man who is known to have entered a virgin's bedroom, clad only in a nightshirt, to steal and secrete a precious jewel, but who has repressed all memory of doing so. The reader will also remember that the initiator of his amnesiac behaviour is eventually revealed to be none other than the family physician, who secretly administered a large dose of opium as a practical joke to pay back the young man for a slur the latter made at the dinner table on the value of medicine.

Throughout the cultural productions of the nineteenth century the same characters, the same images, the same sexual topography recur time and again. Not only in the repetitive and recherché eroticisms of its pornography (works which admit of no frustration) but also in more respectable surrounds: in art, in literature, in architecture, in medical textbooks. Constantly re-interpreted, but constantly returned to, these representations define a terrain of ideal bourgeois masculinity, together with an unspoken realisation that such an ideal is impossible to attain. The aim of this paper is to begin to provide some of the necessary terms for an understanding of that ideal, and to detect in its perverse oppositions some of the contours of the masculine erotic. The examples chosen are from the period of roughly the 1860s to the 1880s – the period before the beginning of England's industrial decline. But the paper does not claim to be a work of historical analysis. It is rather presented in the spirit of an amateur, and taxonomically bogus, Victorian archaeological inquiry, and in the hope that it may provoke resonances, recognitions in a debate about contemporary masculinity.

The representations of male and female thrown up here are not to be seen as 'stereotypical' in a derogatory sense which often carries a meaning of being the opposite of 'real, human beings'. Perhaps they should be thought of rather as the manifestations of psychic problems, necessary productions of historical imperatives, but always surprising in their specificities. For what we have to deal with is not the simple fact that social theorists, popular pundits, medical men and philosophers both sane and demented, chose to attribute, (empirically, they said, yet in spite of the evidences of their senses, we assume) sets of immutable characteristics to 'men' on the one hand, and 'women' on the other. Rather it is the fact that the wisdom of our fathers was able to regard the categories of 'masculine' and 'feminine' as sufficiently distinct sides of a cultural polarity to enable those categories to bear these sets of antinomies. And in that we cannot afford any superior luxury of sniggering at the misconceptions of the past. For not only are those gender attributes of the last century still, to some extent, our tragic legacy, but, more importantly, we live in a culture in which the domestic and erotic potentials are equally frozen along gender lines.

We begin our Cook's tour in Kensington Gardens. A most graphic example of the Victorian age's ideological separation of male and female can be witnessed in the Albert Memorial, that elaboration of 'imaginary architecture' designed and executed by Sir George Gilbert Scott, but commissioned and over-looked at every stage by the symbolic archetype of the repressive bourgeois mother, Queen Victoria, as a monument to her dead lover, the Prince Consort. For those unfamiliar with this ludicrous edifice of pure signification some description is necessary.

The memorial can be broken down into several different components: on an elevated platform approached by steps is a massive canopy rising in the form of a cross, covered with metal-work and jewel-work, and which encloses the gargantuan centrepiece: a statue of the seated consort. Flanking this are two sets of four groups of figures: one set representing the four continents of the world, the other the four useful trades of mankind: commerce, industry, agriculture and engineering. The base is surrounded by reliefs of illuminati from the worlds of painting, sculpture, architecture, poetry and music. There are about 230 individual statues, of which 169 are these named artistic representatives. All but one of these latter, are, of course, masculine – the solitary female being Nitocris, apparently a Queen of Egypt who is said to have built the third pyramid. The other female figures are all allegorical: they represent continents, countries, skills. But most importantly all the figures which flank the spire, like fairies on a Christmas tree, are female: bronze statues of the sciences, Christian and moral virtues and mosaic pictures of allegorical representations of the art. Though *The Times* offered a mild reproach to the Memorial for exiling these virtues 'above roof level' it is highly appropriate to the class mentality of the edifice that the lineaments of femininity should embody the virtues to which the individuated males below should aspire, and that we should have to crane for a glimpse of these qualities whilst the great men on the podium below are the only statues we can approach straight on.

Men aspire, women inspire. But what is perhaps more difficult for us to understand is why all these geniuses, all these virtues, all these continents, all these skills should constellate around the gigantesque epicentre of that supreme nonentity, Albert. And yet, what more natural for the Victorian mentality, which is the parsimonious legacy of those of us blessed to be born Britons, than to include as its ideological foundation a monumental representation of the paterfamilias in a memorial which today seems nothing less than paranoid in its desperate attempts to include a representation of *everything*. For this aristocrat from an obscure German principality and his English spouse fought a crucial ideological crusade against the decadent excesses of the ruling class into which they had been born. Class traitors, they emerged symbolic champions of the puritanical, evangelical bourgeoisie. A populist monarchy in an age when 'the people' was synonomous with the middle-classes they are the structural as well as actual forebears of today's Holy Family of Windsor, with whom Fleet Street reporters imagine us to be so fascinated, and whose antics provide us with a continuing soap-opera of sexual and familial possibilities. This process was inaugurated by Victoria and her spouse, Albert, whose castrating stare looms down at us from that Necropolis in SW1, and who holds in his hand a gigantic book which is (as if to belie the ambitions of the genius men clustered beneath him) a catalogue of the Great Exhibition – the shop-window of capitalist manufacture, the Baedecker of bourgeois consumerism, the A-Z of commodity fetishism.

Let us, before we leave this monument for a humbler destination, imagine its inversion: a memorial in which the continents, the labours, the creative endeavours and the spiritual virtues orbit around a giant bronze statue of a masturbating infant.

We leave London for the northern provinces to examine the operation of this ideological separation between man and woman in a more domestic setting. For in order to spy on that sex which is deemed lawful, licit, we must take particular notice of the theatrical space in which the act of sex is sanctioned to take place: the bourgeois home. We leave the public architecture of the Memorial for the domestic architecture and interior decoration of the successful entrepreneur. Where better to examine the *mise-en-scène* of sanctioned masculine desire than in the household of an architect?

Watson Fothergill was a provincial architect working in Nottingham during the last quarter of the nineteenth century. He built warehouses, offices and civic buildings for the town's bourgeoisie as well as supplying them with expensive villas to live in. However, the bulk of his income was probably derived from property speculation and the sale of land leases for working-class housing. At a time when the Gothic Revival was already on the way out and dismissed by many as old-fashioned, Fothergill continued to design buildings of an eccentric Gothic style, though these designs were divorced from the philosophical implications they carried in the earlier years of the reign. For him the Gothic style was simply 'an inexhaustible supply of novelties'. And yet, when we read in the journals he kept, like so many Victorians, throughout his working life, his views on the design and function of a house and his descriptions of his own suburban villa we find, paradoxically, a more profound philosophy than the mystical aspirations of a Pugin, or the utopian elevation of medieval craft organisation of his more famous contemporary William Morris. More profound, though, only in the sense that its triviality takes us closer to the heart of what the English bourgeoisie of a century ago thought about themselves, how they wished to present themselves to posterity, and how, in defining the home as the domain of woman, they use gender as an ideological structuring device.

For Fothergill the medieval style of architecture was particularly appropriate to achieve a 'home-like effect'. The essence of this effect was individuality: the rampant and outrageous eclectism of his villas was precisely a means of cultivating an individuality of design which would reflect the individuality of the bankers and industrialists who commissioned buildings from him. The necessary implication is that the characterless monotony of working-class streets reflects the lack of individuality, the lack of character of the lower orders. Only a gentleman is allowed to be an individual, only he is able to use his home as a theatrical space of signification. As Fothergill puts it: 'by making too many sacrifices to utilitarianism the nobility of a design will suffer.' In life as in architecture. So the house becomes, in Ruskin's words, 'a kind of monument', a monument to the actual head of the household and to the notion of family life. This is how Fothergill describes the habitation he built for himself and his family:

> The snuggest of houses! This is what we aimed at. Comfort and not great cold rooms, but gems of art sparkling about, an inviting home. As you pass through the vaulted porch into the square hall the merry tinkle of chimes rings on your ear from over the fireplace ... Cast a glance at Lilith with the snake coiled round her ... look at the beams and boarded ceiling overhead; then come into the dining-room, over the arch a stag looks down, having a memory of Ireland attached to it ... the floral decorations over the

arches with mottoes 'He that striveth for mastery is temperate in all things.' (St. Paul.)

After much effusion he ends the description on a note of regret which must have been familiar longing of the Victorian patriarch:

It lacks but age with a few ancestral traditions attached to it to render it more dear to us.

Such is the *mise-en-scène*, what of the dramatis personae? The home is, naturally, the pretended domain of women. The attributes of his five daughters and their accomplishments in music, sketching, Sunday school teaching and sick visiting are enumerated in no less detail than the fixtures and fittings. Surely it is to do no disrepect to his obvious love for them to describe his daughters as 'possessions'? They are written about in a completely different style from that of his two sons – sad disappointment of future possibility. Of the one: 'I hope his business will suit him, but I had desired for him something higher,' and, of the other: '... the black sheep, the miscreant, always in some pickle or other, and always full of some nonsensical tale he is bursting to tell you.' The sons are measured by the roles they can play outside the home, the daughters as ornamentation within it. The daughters are much easier to love, as they only remind the father of the temporality of his ownership at such times as they threaten to become other men's wives. The sons are inherent rivals – it is only right that Papa should demean their competitive potential.

In all this catalogue of expressionistic ornamentation there is, however, one note of criticism:

The adjoining room is Mother's [that is his wife's] ... hence she directs the affairs of the household and controls the back entrance to the house. Strange to say the apartment is hung with architectural prints.

Do we sense a jealousy of professional encroachment? The home is the domain of women, but only to the extent that the 'angel in the house' organises the resuscitation of the bread-winner, depleted from his labours in the jungles of commerce, the world of men. For such function is she placed in charge of the hordes of servants cramped below stairs. Though subordinated through idealistic adoration by her husband, the middle-class lady is nonetheless elevated above the male and female minions whose work ensures the reproduction of the household as theatre, and as microcosm of the outside world.

If she can withstand an adolescent apprenticeship of demure triviality, if she can surmount a period of soul-deadening, hysteria-inducing ennui, then, after a bloody *rite de passage*, she is promised to become, like her husband, a Boss. She must then put aside the childish frivolities which were her outlet as a daughter, and, with the Janus-mask of respectability, rule the home: one sweet aspect facing outward, the social secretary and lady-in-waiting to the master; another face, somewhat less angelic, that of manageress of the 'back entrance'. She, like he, is born to rule.

Here is Fothergill's final summation of the function of the house:

> Yes. This is the head-quarters where we sit and criticise often most mercilessly the rest of the world and one another. We unbuckle our armour here, we have no secrets within our home. We can all trust one another that keen as may be the darts shot at each other here, yet when outside in the world the family shows a bold front and wards off from its members any arrows aimed from a foreign bow.

So in the family home no less than at the Albert Memorial we are in the domain of sexual classification, the body of the sexes is suborinated to and organised around furnishings. But if the operation of power functions to define sex as licit or illicit then this detour through domestic architecture should be enough to convince us that, for a body of Victorian opinion, working-class sexuality is inherently illicit. Not only those outrageous pundits who prescribed sterilisation as cure for the genetically transmitted disease of pauperism, but also more reformist mentalities make us suspect this. The 'social explorers' into working-class areas of Darkest England, the abyss, report back with horror on the licentiousness of their objects of study. It seems as if their shock at seeing for themselves the way in which the forces of capital had constrained its reservoir of surplus value is, in part, predicated upon the spectre of incest. If power splits sex into the licit and the illicit then we should not be surprised to see this reflected spatially in the topographical conditions which surround the act. When capital finished with the productive capacity of its workers, male and female, when old and drained the miserable couple were forced upon the resources of the state to pass their twilight days picking oakum and eating gruel, once again the disavowal of working-class sexuality came into operation by dividing the man from the woman at the workhouse gate, and allowing them visual access to each other only at chapel.

If the working class sprawl promiscuously all over one another, defying every canon of classification, and the angel remains securely in the house as stage manageress and licensed glory-hole for the paterfamilias, where and in what guise do we seek the son, young Oedipus? The ambivalent adolescent, locus of jealous possessions for the ageing father, must serve a long and exacting apprenticeship before he is allowed to pose in the wedding portrait. His sexuality hedged in and regarded from all sides – his youthful penis strapped each night into the spiked urethal ring or the electric alarum to warn him of his nocturnal erections; his public school a topographical and ideological bastion against the debilitating excesses of the solitary vice, the loss of the vital Empire-building fluid; his life in the regiment or in training for business or the professions organised to keep him from the company of those angelic creatures who haunt his thoughts. He must walk a sexual tightrope whilst accumulating the economic wherewithal necessary, in his thirties, to slip into the shoes of his father.

For this psychic torture on the road to eventual class and race domination he is offered some small compensation, a romantic image to hold in his mind as he is sent out into the Empire: the image of the Christian knight, Sir Gawain, the Happy Warrior. The schoolboy knight reaches his apotheosis in Sir John Everett Millais' painting *The Knight Errant*, which hangs in the Tate. In his gleaming silver armour this

fresh-faced youth with straight nose and set jaw looks like
nothing less than the Captain of the 1st XI sent out into the
dark world by Dr Arnold on his first mission past the confines
of the quad. He straddles the thick trunk of what appears to be
a birch tree which divides the picture along its vertical axis. On
the left hand side of the frame bound to this trunk is a young
maiden totally naked, her knee length hair making no attempt
to hide her nudity, her flimsy garments trailing out of the
corner of the image. The young hero has his sword drawn and
the painting surprises him in the act of cutting through her
bonds; the sword, in the centre of the frame – rubbing
alongside the trunk of the tree so that their figures are divided
by both sword and tree which splits the frame in half. Behind
them is the landscape of a dark, almost abstract wood, the
crescent moon as source of light in the top left hand corner,
the damsel's side of the composition. In opposition to that in
the top corner of the knight's side of the frame, barely
discernible, easily mistaken for trees, are two figures, brown
strokes on the canvas, their arms in the air fleeing from the
scene.

The resonances of this fetishistic image are acute enough
today, but the story goes that when exhibited in the Academy,
it was severely criticised and berated for its obvious sensuality.
Millais had to change the painting before it was sold, four
years later, to Sir Henry Tate. The change he made was
astounding: we are told that in the original picture the naked
maiden looked straight out of the frame at the spectator.[2] In
the picture which stands before us now her head is turned
away, her eyes cast down in shame, she appears, as Millais' son
put it, 'altogether more modest'.

As the picture now stands the eye-line of the Christian
knight appears to connect with nothing – it is as if he is looking
out of frame rather than concentrating on cutting the bonds.
In the original, presumably, his gaze would have hit the face of
the maiden, whose own gaze was directed out at us. Like the
knight, the spectators at the Academy would have been faced
with the fact of sexual difference – meeting a gaze which
betrayed no shame. Face to face with the possibility of
castration – the sword strokes the tree-trunk rooted between

The Knight Errant, Sir John Everett Millais

man and woman but belonging to either – they turned in
despair and ran, like the varlets disappearing from the top
right hand corner. And with the knowledge of this change
when we again look at his face we see, not youthful resolve and
determination, but a contained unblinking horror. From now
on, we speculate, this stainless young hero will be drained of
his manliness – he will never re-conquer fear. His gaze has met
the gaze of the Other, try as he might he will never completely
recover the world of men. Let him run to the North West
frontier and confront the savage; let him lord it over the
tenants on his estate, it will be of no avail. The spectre of
castration has produced another dread victim of
spermatorrhea.

There is little need to document in any detail this invented
disease of 'involuntary sexual emission', it has been well
written about elsewhere.[3] Suffice it to say that, once again, as in
the joke with which we began, the medical authorities have
provided a taxonomical guarantee for the physiological reality
of sexual anxiety. Stephen Heath is quite right to suggest that
the 'determining' factor behind the 'invention' of this disease
and the numerous alarming devices designed to warn the
youth that he is victim of it 'is not in the first instance any
design of repression but the approach to the sexual as an
impossible economy of physiological balance'. However,
beyond this 'first instance' lies the unmistakable mechanisms
of a particular strategy of repression operating as regards the
articulation of this terrible affliction with the practice of
masturbation. It is important to remember that spermatorrhea
and masturbation are not reducible to one another. The
former is a disease, the latter is a 'vile practice'. So infant,
childhood and adolescent masturbation, which can be a cause
of later spermatorrhea (along with 'youthful indiscretion,
libidinous thoughts, highly seasoned food, stimulating
beverages', but the list is endless as each expert had his own
ideas on the subject) is a vice which is not only widely prevalent
('it has been rightly said that ninety-nine out of a hundred boys
of this depraved generation engage in this vile practice and the
other one-in-a-hundred conceals the truth' said one American
authority) but also necessary to repress as masturbation is

voluntary – a triumph of the will.

If masturbation represents a vile democratic aspiration of vice to which all male children are subject, then spermatorrhea, as Heath points out, is a class-specific disease primarily afflicting 'barristers, medical men, authors, tutors, clergymen', exactly those young Knights of Empire deprived of all but the most constrained female contact whilst in the liminal zones of apprenticeship. It is as if our young heroes had to start a sexuality from scratch on their wedding nights, a night on which their demure young prizes were advised to obey the mythical injunctions of their mothers to 'lie back and think of England'. (Are we, by the way, to interpret this exhortation as a substitution on a metaphorical level – the thought of the glorious homeland standing in to protect against the possibility of other, more degrading thoughts which might be stimulated by the act in which the young virgin is about to participate with her passivity – or as a substitution on a metonymical level – this novel, sanctioned lover as England's representative in this act; thus, to think of England is to think of her husband as the Empire's embodiment?)

It is, therefore, tempting to see the exigencies of sexual economy overlapping entirely with the demands of political economy. No wonder so many thrusting entrepreneurs of the mid-century were disappointed with the namby-pamby male offspring who, brought up in a life of luxury, had no spirit left for taking the helm of the family firm. No wonder that if the father postponed for so long any possibility of a resolution of the Oedipus complex then he later found to his regret that it could never be resolved, the Lord would not intervene to restore his Isaac. The architect Forthergill, for example, in an entry in his journal eight years after the one previously quoted, writes of his son:

> After consultations with doctors it became too evident that the delusions which were always in his mind rendered it necessary that he should be under constant supervision ... and I took him to an asylum. This is a terrible affliction for us all. His mental derangement was caused by his own evil habits.

Can you be so sure, father as you wash your hands of the black sheep? Are you not aware that one of the prime causes of self-pollution in youth is 'perverted amativeness'? 'Yes,' says Dr Orson Squire Fowler, 'this is inherited by many children. It is the result of the lust and licentiousness of one or both parents during the child's prenatal life.'

Truly an 'impossible sexuality' whose perverse consequences are ironically celebrated in this underground hymn to the disease:

Our pallid complexions foreshadow deaths doom in us
And our water's remarkably thick and albuminous,
Nocturnal emissions o'erwhelm us in oceans,
And at stool our roes shoot along with our motions.
Spermatorrhea
That's what we fear,
We shall all perish from spermatorrhea.[4]

So the bourgeois parents acting under doctor's orders in the interests of economy, do not allow the future administrators of the imperialist state a sexual imagination. Though we can speculate that the montage of thoughts guiltily flooding the minds of their offspring whilst they secretly flog their members in the dorm are constrained, even determined by the very power-structure which refuses them permission to wet-dream through these thoughts to solitary orgasm. The limited set of characters, dialogue, situations we stumble upon in Victorian pornography is witness to this social production of perversity. Is this then the paradox at the heart of the issue: does the exercise of social power determine, categorise and produce the set of sexual possibility within which members of a society must operate? Or is the erotic, no matter whether exercised respectably in the middle-class bedroom or peasant cottage, or perversely in the adolescent cot or urban slum, always in excess of social demands?

To decide in favour of either side leads to an impasse: to say 'yes' to the former means all of us must be complicit with the limiting of our sexual possibilities and put them in abeyance until such time as we have changed society, or someone else has changed it for us, at which time the movement of desire will, with our full consent, automatically change. To say 'yes' to the latter is to underwrite our society's evaluation, whether in progressive or reactionary guise, of sex as the secret garden in which essential nature will always contrive to cover over the pruning exercises of a rational species. Sex becomes a place apart, a Highgate Cemetery of the personality, where strangling weeds make mockery of all our attempt to control the memory of ourselves as good, clean citizens. Therefore we should succumb to its natural and essential domination. And yet these two options are what seem to be available in most of the discourses surrounding sexuality. Perhaps this is the crux of Foucault's third point quoted at the beginning of this paper – power's hold on sex is maintained through the act of discourse which creates a rule of law. What does that mean? That we can challenge power in the discourses produced around sex by challenging the fixity of those discourses? Can this be enough?

Many a sexual commentator in the last few years, for instance, has taken on the erotic monument of the Victorian era, *My Secret Life*, pseudonymously and privately published by an unknown writer 'Walter'.[5] Indeed, the discourses which surround the work threaten to become as multi-layered as the text itself. The identity of the author of this class of sexual literature remains unknown, but we can infer much about his attitudes and class position from the text he left. This largely unread monument, available in this country only in versions of a greater or lesser degree of abridgment, is a blow-by-blow account of the encounters of an upper-middle-class gentleman who was 'only interested in one thing' – commentators disagree as to whether that thing is the most important thing in the world or not. Like Fothergill, and countless others of his age, he was concerned to memorialise his life in writing – though for what audience apart from himself, is a matter of conjecture. It is clear from the title of the book that the world on display here is one which is ignored in the Victorian novel, but one which existed in parallel to that of the 'respectable' domestic sexual economy of a Fothergill. That world is, of course, the 'sexual underground', a world in which, like its more seemly counterpart, any commodity is available to the man of means.

The style of the book is remarkable in that Walter re-wrote his memories from detailed notes jotted down shortly after the experiences took place. To this end it little resembles the structure and style of the majority of works of nineteenth century pornography, with their endless ritualised beatings and fetishistic and purple-prosed metaphors of sexual anatomy. Instead it allows a fascinating insight into the methodology, economics and language of Victorian prostitution and sexuality in general. Walter's desire for 'authentic' representation of his life, his failures as well as his successes, his anxieties as well as his triumphs, tells us much about Victorian attitudes towards the human body, male and female, and the management of the sexual sphere. Because of his desire not only to re-live his experiences through writing (the act of memory and putting it down on paper are the specific erotic residues to which the reader is privy), but also, purportedly, to educate and inform the youth of a repressive society about the 'naturalness' of their sexual longings (Walter's medical pretensions), the book remains a valuable document.

However, we must be wary of over-evaluating the apparently 'progressive' aspects of a life which flouted the taboos of a rigid moral code. Though Walter's encounters took place with women of all classes, 'from a marchioness to well-nigh a beggar', nevertheless the majority of them were conducted with servants, whom he used his position to seduce, and prostitutes, procured with his inherited wealth. So although Walter says that 'fucking is the great humanizer of the world', removing all social distinctions between a man and a woman, the financial remunerations which accompany his encounters so often belie this. Indeed, it is almost as if Walter could not successfully conclude a sexual transaction unless the 'spending' of his vital fluid was accompanied and balanced by a financial loss. Let us very briefly review the responses to this extraordinary document from a 'more enlightened' age.

Discourse piles upon discourse, commentary upon commentary.[6] For Doctors Eberhard and Phyllis Kronhausen, for example, (who, as their Scandinavian nomenclature suggests, speak from a perspective of 60s American sexology and sexual therapy, 'a positive position on sexuality') Walter is a sexual radical with 'little hostility' towards women in comparison to most self-aggrandising Don Juans, and an 'enthusiasm' for female anatomy. To Fraser Harrison, on the other hand, Walter is little more than a rapist using his class position as a means of seducing working women whom he treats as 'insensate physical extensions of his own cerebral longings'. Steven Marcus, in the first and by far the fullest account of the book, summarises Walter as essentially self-centred, 'a representative figure of cultural subversion in his own time, he representatively anticipates what is to become the conformity of ours' in the sense that Walter's desire for sexual change is completely divorced from any notion of social change, unlike his male and female contemporaries. For Michel Foucault, Walter as a producer of discourse about sex 'serves better than his Queen as the central figure for a sexuality' (of his period). Finally, for Stephen Heath, Walter's unending and repetitive quest for sex is 'cast in the mould of the science of the age, a succession of observations and practical experiments' whose main search for knowledge is the confirmation of sexual difference: 'What does Walter want to know: The female sex, 'the woman', to be sure of *her*, that is, of himself, of his identity as a man.'

Well, yes, all of these things – some more than others ... perhaps. And yet what is finally in excess of any of them is the fact of the text. Is it that writing is in excess of the loveless and impoverished sexuality that is its subject matter? Or is it that the subject of a man's sexuality transforms the act of writing, turns the book into a chimera as we try and grasp it?

I will confine myself to only one quotation from this massive book, and one which, in terms of its literary style is far from representative of the book as a whole, owing more to imitation of the pornography of the time than Walter's more usual 'down-to-earth' diary style:

Why is it that after I have made love to a thousand vaginas, another vagina, because unknown, untasted and fresh proves to be so irresistible?

(this is Heath's question in Walter's own words, the necessity to confirm continually the fact of sexual difference, of his own interpellation as a man)

> It destroys resolve, frustrates determination, causes me weakly to yield to its charms and makes me want to enter it.

(echoes here in the description of the effects of sex of the symptoms of spermatorrhea)

> though I am certain as I look and feel it that it will give me no more delight by friction, grip and suction than hundreds of the others that my prick has tasted

(the bitter turn of masculinity, the impossibility of closure, the story without an ending)

> Verily, vagina is queen, king, emperor, high-priest, commander-in-chief, an army in itself, a necromancer, a wizard, a saint of marvellous power – all these and more. Who can withstand it? Why not yield to it?

(Strange, isn't it, that after granting this organ the position of 'queen' that all subsequent metaphors have masculine connotations?)

It is tempting to look at this passage in the light of Freud's second contribution to the psychology of love, 'On the Universal Tendency to Debasement in the Sphere of Love.'[7] In this essay he considers the disorder he was most often asked to treat – impotence,

> a refusal of the executive organs of sexuality to carry out the sexual act

and, without wishing to do violence to the subtlety of his reasoning, concludes that

> the strange failure shown in psychical impotence makes its appearance whenever an object which has been chosen with the aim of avoiding incest recalls the prohibited object through some

feature, often an inconspicuous one.

The memory of the Mother, rather than the word 'No', proves to be the best form of contraception. The protection to which many men have recourse in an attempt to avoid this embarrassing psychical disturbance consists of a debasement of the sexual object – there must be no possibility in the manifestation of his masculinity that the object of affection for our poor hero may carry any connotations of that huge, pure and terrifying female who brought him into the world. But there is a further sting in the tail as the fantasies of the young boy in a pre-adolescent state, when he has gained 'a more or less complete knowledge of the sexual relations between adults', turn on the similarity between the mother and the whore, in order to provide the pre-condition of her allowing a sexual access to the child, which she reserves for the father. Though the adult male runs to the company of women who, because he regards them as socially and morally inferior, will not threaten his ability to perform, he can never be sure that he will out-pace the fantasy – the signifiers of incest may at any moment have their castrating revenge on the body of the young Don Juan. Male sexuality is at best an unpredictable business for these limp patients of the doctor. But Freud is not content to leave it at that: it is not just to a few unfortunate souls that the above scenario pertains;

> Since we must recognise that all the relevant factors known to us – the strong childhood fixation (to the mother), the incest-barrier and the frustration in the years of development after puberty – are to be found in practically all civilised human beings, we should be justified in expecting psychical impotence to be a universal affliction under civilisation and not a disorder confined to some individuals.

The tragic definition of a 'civilised' man's sexuality lies in his inability to perform at will. We are defined as men by our impotence, the limp penis as symbol of our sex.

In this light we see Walter's relentless seduction of servants, his profligate consumption of prostitutes not as a quixotic attempt to break down class-barriers through the conduit of the genitals, but rather as the furious retreat from the body of the Mother, of which women of his own class threaten to remind him. This seems to be confirmed by his attitude to his despised wife, the 'missus', the 'old woman', constantly presented as a detestable tyrant whose role is to deny him the possibility of pleasure. The home, for him, is a site of inhibition, not, as for Fothergill, a place of recuperation.

Freud's pessimistic conclusion, that 'something in the nature of the sexual instinct itself is unfavourable to the realisation of complete satisfaction' seems to be confirmed in Walter's hopeless project to rid himself of his class-determined inhibitions:

> the final object of the sexual instinct is never any longer the original object, but only a surrogate for it. Psychoanalysis has shown us that when the original object of a wishful impulse has been lost as a result of repression it is frequently represented by an endless series of subsitutive objects none of which, however, brings full satisfaction.

And yet, there is still something in Walter's unsophisticated prose which revolts against the sophistication of Freud's explanation. There is still, however disingenuous an attitude of resistance against sexual taboos, even though his actions ultimately confirmed rather than challenged the inequities of the social world he inhabited. There is still something about Walter's degrading question, which is, at least, more 'modern' than Fothergill's beautiful architectural sublimations. Perhaps it is simply a pretended illusion he shares with us: that we can change our sexuality.

Part of Walter's life-project, explorer that he was, to cross the sexual frontiers of the age, was to conquer his fears about, and his initial repugnance towards homosexual connection, to break the barriers of what he regards as a socially conditioned taboo. And yet, when he achieves this aim he is first anxious to ascertain from the young man who is to be his partner that he is not a 'sodomite' – his desire is to screw a heterosexual man a man who, like himself, loves women. And yet, when the encounter is over he pays this unemployed carpenter with the gold he has inherited, the same gold with which he buys his women. And yet ... and yet ...

We end near where we began, under the domination of a sexuality categorised for us and by us as respectable or perverse, as focus of anxiety or liberation, as the placid mirror of social power or its anarchic challenger. And we return again to that most persistent, most 'natural' of polarities: the opposition between 'man' and the 'woman'. Before we leave the nineteenth century to renegotiate the specific knife-edge we balance one hundred years later, let us consider the ideological immutibility of gender separation with which we are faced in the first verse of a poem by Rudyard Kipling: 'The Ballad of East and West.' The first line of this poem is well known as an exemplar of colonial racism, blueprint for imperial domination.

Oh East is East and West is West and never the twain shall meet

The second line builds on this and confirms it:

Till Earth and Sky stand presently at God's great judgement seat,

the difference between the cultures of the east and those of the west is as 'natural' as that between the earth and the sky, and it is impossible to imagine them uniting whilst the world as we know it still exists. So far, so straightforward. However, the immutability of this separation is challenged in the second couplet, which begins with a massive 'but':

But there is neither East nor West, Border nor Breed nor Birth

What is it that can challenge all the assumptions of the masters of the earth? What is it that can dissolve the distinctions of race, nationality and class? The answer is in the last line:

When two strong men stand face to face, tho' they come from the ends of the earth.

The fact of masculinity remains when all other social categories have disappeared, indeed it is the agent of their disappearance. The 'strong man' looks in the face of the Other and recognises himself – but only when that Other, stripped of the signifiers of class and race, is seen to be of the same gender. For did not the same poet tell us that 'The Colonel's Lady and Judy O'Grady are sisters under the skin.' Notice here, however, that the essential similiarity between the 'female of the species' is evidenced by recourse to two representatives which, though taken from opposite ends of a social spectrum, remain nonetheless white. Masculinity is more pervasive ... or perhaps more vulnerable: how would Millais have painted the expression if on a quest in the moonlit wood his knight errant had come across the naked body of a Maharajah or Zulu chieftain strapped to the tree? Where would he have placed the sword?

For this is the White Man's Burden: to drag around the deserts, jungles, mountain ranges and wildernesses of the world this unaccountable organ, whose unwelcome tumescences are always accompanied with stabs of acute pain, whose unpredictable swellings ring the alarum bell in the psyche, only to return with the spoils to the centre of the Empire and find, alone on the wedding night in the presence of an unveiled angel, it is the only organ in his body not rigid with terror. This vicious circle in which we serve – the Boys who've lost an Empire and haven't found a role.

References

1 *The Pearl* – a journal of facetiae and voluptuous reading; No. 18, December 1880, reprinted by The Grove Press 1968.
2 The painting is discussed in relation to the Victorian rediscovery of chivalry in Mark Girouard, *The Return to Camelot*, Yale University Press 1981.
3 See the recent discussions in Jeffrey Weeks, *Sex, Politics and Society*, Longman 1981, and Stephen Heath, *The Sexual Fix*, Macmillan 1982.
4 Poem by G.A. Sala reproduced in Peter Fryer, *The Man of Pleasures Companion*, Arthur Baker 1968.
5 A relatively unabridged paperback version of *My Secret Life* was published by Grove Press in 1966.

6 Walter is discussed in Doctors Eberhard and Phylis Kronhausen, *Walter – the English Casanova*, Polybooks 1967, Fraser Harrison, *The Dark Angel*, Fontana 1979, Steven Marcus, *The Other Victorians*, Weidenfield and Nicholson 1966, Foucault, op. cit. and Heath op. cit.

7 In Volume 7 of the Penguin Freud Library. I am grateful to Claire Johnston for reminding me of the pertinence of this essay.

Notes on Contributors

Angela Carter's first novel, *Shadow Dance*, was published in 1965, while her second, *The Magic Toyshop* won the John Llewellyn Rhys Prize in 1967 and her most recent, *The Passion of New Eve*, was published in 1977. Her journalism has appeared in almost every major British publication, and her poetry has been published in the *Listener* and *London Magazine*.

Jon Cook works in the school of English and American Studies at the University of East Anglia, where he is an active member of ASTMS. Author of *Romanticism and Ideology* (1981), he has also published articles on cultural studies and post-romantic literature.

Zelda Curtis has both written and worked for *Labour Monthly*, the *Morning Star* and *East End News*; for many years a member of the Communist Party, she is now a member of the Labour Party.

Michael Eaton works as an independent film-maker and a teacher of Film Studies at Leicester Polytechnic. A contributor to a number of film magazines and a member of *Screen*'s editorial board, he is the editor of *Anthropology – Reality – Cinema* (1979), a study of the French film-maker Jean Rouch. His article in this book is based on his research for his third film, *Darkest England* about Victorian upper-class masculinity.

Noël Greig was a co-founder of the Combination Arts Lab (originally of Brighton, later Deptford), and subsequently worked with various theatre groups, including Inter-Action,

Oval House and Gay Sweatshop. His plays have been widely performed and a number of them, including *The Dear Love of Comrades* (1981) and *As Time Goes By* (1981), co-authored with Drew Griffiths, published. He is currently working on a biography of Edward Carpenter.

Eileen Phillips teaches at the City of London Polytechnic where she is completing research on the impact of new technology on women and office work. Active in the Communist Party and the Women's Liberation Movement, she is a member of the *Feminist Review* editorial collective, and has written for a wide range of magazines and journals, from *Marxism Today* to *Computing* and *Scarlet Woman* to *New Musical Express*.

Frankie Rickford has been active in the women's liberation movement in Bristol and London for ten years. Before her present job on NALGO's journal she was a reporter for the *Morning Star*, and is an occasional contributor to *Marxism Today*, *Spare Rib* and *City Limits*. She is a member of the support group of Lewisham Women's Aid and also teaches Re-evaluation Co-counselling. She is 29.

Michèle Roberts was Poetry Editor of *Spare Rib* between 1974 and 1976 and of *City Limits* between 1981 and 1983. She is co-author of four collections of poetry and one of short stories, *Tales I Tell My Mother* (1978). She has published two novels, *A Piece of the Night* (1978) and *The Visitation* (1983), and is currently working on a third, *The Wild Girl*. She performs her work regularly at music and cabaret events, and also teaches creative writing at the City Lit and in London schools.

Elizabeth Wilson trained and worked as a psychiatric social worker and now teaches social studies at the Polytechnic of North London. She has worked and written for a number of magazines and journals, including *Case Con, Critical Social Policy, Red Rag* and *Feminist Review*. Her most recent books are *Mirror Writing* (1982) and *What Is To Be Done About Violence Against Women?* (1983), and she is currently writing a book on fashion.